What people are

"Whether or not you grew up experiencing an earthly father's love, this book will introduce you the greatest love of all ... that of our Heavenly Father. John provides insight into the many facets of God's love for us and helps us to understand how to more fully experience that love."

John, I count it a privilege to have you as friend and brother in Christ. You are a living testimony of how the Father's love can totally transform a person ... all you need is a little faith .... like a mustard seed!

Blessings, Mark Shumaker

Over the past 10 years, as John and I have ministered shoulder to shoulder to men in the marketplace, I have witnessed firsthand his growth from a newly committed Christ-follower into the mature man of faith he is today. A Father's Love provided for me a superstructure on which to hang the details of John's spiritual progression.

Drawing on his knowledge of the Scriptures together with his experiences – good and bad - with his father and stepfather and as a father of five himself, John has attained a profound understanding of the father-son relationship that God has entered into with all believers. Out of this understanding has taken root a trust in God as a father who only wants what is best for his children that has produced in John the deep love relationship with the Lord that governs his life today.

Through reading the book I found myself being drawn into the heart of this selfless God who longs for me truly to know him as my "Father." What's more, I was challenged to "buck up" my own testimony of this relationship, and the examples John includes in the book of ways he himself has done this helped me.

I highly recommend <u>A Father's Love</u> to both believer and seeker, to both those desiring to deepen their love for their Heavenly Father and those still exploring the Christian faith.

Jim Furr

A FATHERS' LOVE

BY JOHN ROBERTSON

Dylan,

Your Father Loves You!,

John Robertson

2 Thess. 3:5

www.TotalPublishingAndMedia.com

Cover design and graphics by Garry Townsley of Grace
Works and The Graphic Design and Operations teams at Total
Publishing and Media.

ISBN: 978-0-88144-189-5

TABLE OF CONTENTS

ACKNOWLEDGMENTS

It seems necessary to dedicate this to the Father who inspired and encouraged me to write this book because of His Love, He who knows me better than anyone, and knew what I needed to know about Him, in order for me to become the kind of father He created me to be. I would also like to dedicate it to my family, my wife of twenty four years who has faithfully supported me in all my endeavors, and to my children who know all too well, that I have not been as good a father as I should have been. Also to my precious grandchildren who constantly remind me of what love is all about. I'm sure there are more reasons and purposes in the writing of this book than I know, but I'm sure of at least one of them; That I might better understand the nature and characteristics of a Father's Love, in order to help me become the husband, father and grandfather that I was created to be. I also dedicate it to my father, stepfather, mother, stepmothers, aunts, uncles and other family members who have been an important part in who I've become, as well as the many men and women that the Father has placed in my life to help me better know Him. Also to my Pastors and church family, thanks to all of you who have been a part of my life, there are far too many to name.

I would also like to dedicate it to all the fathers, mothers and children who will read it and hopefully better understand their Father's love and love for each other.

INTRODUCTION

T his book is written about The Father's love, which I believe is widely misunderstood today. The Bible, which is the written word of God, written by men who were inspired by and led by God to write this story of A Father's Love for His children, makes this statement, "And abide faith, hope, love, these three; but the greatest of these is love." (1Corinthians 13:13) If it is the greatest of these, which I believe are three essential keys to life, both in this life and in the eternal life to come, therefore it is probably good that we know and understand love, more particularly the love of **the Father** for His children.

As a father myself of five girls, I love them but my love for them was far short of what God intended when He gave them to me. I was busy and distracted like many dads and even moms are. The truth is, I was not equipped to be even a good dad, much less the father I was meant to be. Until, I knew the love of the **Father** Who is the **God** and **Father** of the **Lord Jesus Christ**. I was at best an average father who didn't know much about love, I knew what I felt in my heart, but I failed to show my children what a father's love should be like.

When Jesus began His ministry, He talked about His Father God and about their relationship, He said things like, "If you've seen Me you've seen the Father." He said, "I and My Father are one." He said, "The words that I speak to you I do not speak on My own authority; but the Father who dwells in Me does the works." The Lord put in my heart to write this book from the perspective of A Father's Love for His children.

In doing this I saw the Love of God in a new way, realizing that I am His son because of what He did for me through His Son Jesus, I began to investigate God's love for His children as recorded in the Bible. In this I discovered how inadequate my love for my children is and had been, but I found hope in that now that I have received His love for myself, I am more able and equipped to love them like I have been loved.

Whether you are a man or women, parent or child, most of us have struggled with relationships in our lives. I believe you will learn more about what it is to have and experience and incredible relationship between A Real Father and child as you look at the evidence through out the Bible of His love for His children, in looking at what He did for His children, I saw what I should do as a father for my children and what I cannot do He can and will.

Chapter One

Fathers Want to Know and Be Known by Their Children (Relationships)

R ecently, when my wife and I were babysitting our two grandchildren, a fact stood out to me which I had known before, but I hadn't really given much thought to it: Women have a natural ability to sense what a baby needs.

Unfortunately, this sense doesn't seem to come naturally to men.

On that particular morning, I was holding my grandson, who was congested, and not feeling well. He was not at all comfortable in my arms. My wife Gina kept giving me instructions about what he wanted and needed. I realized she seemed to know just what he wanted. She said, "He doesn't like to lie back too far because he can breathe better in a more upright position." So, I raised him up, and he seemed much happier. Then he grabbed his pacifier out of his mouth and threw it on the floor. Trying to help, I offered him a yogurt snack, but again, I was wrong. Gina said, "He wants his milk!" As I said, women have a natural sense to know just what a child needs and wants!

In much the same way, God, the Father of all, knows what each of us needs and wants. You may wonder, if that's the case, why doesn't He just provide it for us, like mothers do for their children? I believe it's because He desires to know us through relationship. He certainly wants us to have good things and to avoid troubles, but the truth is He knows our nature! He knows that if we get everything we need and want just handed to us, we will become like spoiled children. We'll expect it and not even realize our need for our Father. We would probably become so self-focused that we would never recognize our need to know the Father who is responsible for not only all we have, but even our very existence.

The Bible is full of stories of God, throughout many years and generations, continually supplying the needs of His people, often miraculously. Yet, the more He did for His children, the more they wanted from Him, often not even asking Him for provision, or thanking Him for what He had already provided. They wanted someone else to communicate for them, such as a king, or a priest, or a judge: anyone but them. They acted like my oneyear old grandson who didn't ask for anything because he hadn't learned how, so he cried and threw things to get what he wanted. In much the same way, these people wouldn't ask their Father God for their every need.

We are often much like them today. Just like the people of old, we only call on God when we are in some sort of desperate situation. We teach our children to say "please" and "thank you" as they grow up and eventually they learn this is the best way to get their needs met. Yet, when it comes to our relationship with our Heavenly Father, many of us just expect our needs to be met, not even asking as we should, nor really appreciating God's constant provision.

Have you ever stopped to reflect on how many miracles may have occurred in your life or the lives of your family members over the years? Over time, we often begin to take provision and even miracles for granted, as though these blessings just happen for us. Even worse, sometimes we think we deserve them, that we're better off than others because, after all, we're "good people." We think, "I've always been a good person. I don't treat people unfairly, don't lie, don't steal, don't covet, I attend church regularly, etc."

The truth is we all need the Father! Some of us may recognize our need more than others, but the truth is we *all* need our Father. Listen to what God told His people in Hosea 4:6, "My people are destroyed for a lack of knowledge. Because you have rejected knowledge, I will also reject you from being priest for Me." There are two principles in operation here, and these principles are what the people actually rejected. First, knowledge was available to them (and is, to us), but the people rejected it (just like many of us today). Secondly, people won't become who they should become (or, fulfill God's purposes in their lives) when they reject knowledge! *In other words, God is saying, "There are consequences to your decision to reject the knowledge I have available for you."*

Years ago, after I had already turned my life over to the Lord, I began experiencing some difficulties in my business, kinds of problems I hadn't experienced before. Throughout all my years in business, I rarely had any difficulty with customers, so these problems were new to me! I thought, *"How can this be? Finally, I am living the way I'm supposed to live and now troubles come! What is going on?"*

You could say I haven't always been a "fast" learner. I now found myself in some situations I'm sure the Lord didn't intend for me to get into. In the midst of these problems, my wife confided our situation to her hairdresser, a devout woman, who knew the Lord. She said something I hadn't considered, *"Maybe the Lord is showing you how to recognize a certain type of person, so you can avoid, these kind of situations in the future."* I believe she was right, at least partially. However, there was even more I needed to learn. I struggled through several more of these kinds of troubles, and suffered significant financial loss, before I learned an important principle.

The Lord wanted me to see that I was to consult Him *before* taking a job. Not every job was intended for me, just because it was available. While I did learn some valuable lessons in these situations, I do not believe it was His intended will for me to take all those jobs that had caused me the frustration and loss.

The truth is I was trusting Him with parts of my life, but not even acknowledging Him in other parts. I might as well have said to Him, *"I've got this covered. I am smart enough to handle this. I don't need your help now; I'll let you know when I do."* I didn't realize what I was doing, but I was choosing when I needed to seek God and hear from Him.

This may not seem so bad to you, but it is prideful in His eyes. Proverbs 3:6 says, *"In all your ways acknowledge Him, and He shall direct your path."* Notice, this verse does not say in *some* of your ways acknowledge Him, however, that was precisely what I was doing. God wanted *constant* relationship with me, not just *part-time*. The previous verse, Proverbs 3:5, says, *"Trust in the Lord with all your heart and lean not on your own understanding."* Notice, it also says *all* your heart, not *some*. God was telling me, *"Don't think you are so smart. You're not, so don't trust in what you know, trust in Me because I really know what's best."* Wow! What a revelation! Like I said, I'm not always a fast learner.

Let's apply the two principles I mentioned earlier to the situation I just described. First, knowledge was available. I rejected it by simply not asking God if I should take those jobs. Secondly, those jobs didn't produce the nearly the income that other jobs could have produced. However, God, even in the mess of my own making, used it to teach me about Him and, what is more important, He taught me about myself. He showed me that I have the tendency to take control of things on my own. When

I gave my heart to the Lord, I asked Him to be the Lord of my life. I said, *"I believe You are God and that I need You,"* but then I went right back to relying on myself and my ways. My actions showed that evidently, I was only willing to give Him a part of my life.

Perhaps you can relate to the following, what I call "one-way" prayers. You know, ones like this: *"God bless me, and this day, and all that I do, and thanks for watching over my family."* I used to pray these, kind of prayers. My point is that a "one-way" prayer comes from a one-way relationship and is not an appropriate prayer. Let's consider how that prayer might sound in a two-way relationship, where God is God, my Heavenly Father, and I'm His child. I believe it would be something like this: *"Father God, I love You. I know I'm not capable of doing anything good without You. I need You. I know You have a plan today for me. Thank You for that plan. Help me to be sensitive to Your voice this day so that I can do what You would have me do. Show me how to be a better husband, father, son, friend, brother, and businessperson today. Thank You for hearing my prayer today, In Jesus' name I pray, Amen."*

If you were God, which one would you prefer to hear? Relationships are two-way. They never work any other way; they cannot exist without at least two parties, and they both must be able to communicate. It is through relationship that you really get to know someone. An introduction is a start. You tell one another your name. (If you're like me, you might have to ask their name one or two more times!) It takes time and a genuine effort to get to know someone.

For example, you may have a particular service provider, like a mechanic or a hairdresser, whose services you prefer. You may go several times before even remembering their name. If you continue going for months or even years, you'll probably get to know more about them. Yet that is not enough to really know them. You would still have to engage in conversation, asking questions and then really listening to get to know them. It is no different with God. We need to go to Him in conversation (prayer requests, praise, worship) and we need to seek Him by asking His will and listening for His response, just like you would with someone else.

You may be thinking, *"Why? Why do I need to go to Him in prayer, and why do I need to seek His will for me? If something is God's will, won't it just happen?"* Truthfully, there are more answers than I can list, but in short, it is to complete you. God the Father is the One who created you. He has gifted you in unique ways that only He knows. Only He knows your individual purpose, both why and what He created you to do. It is He who must show you your place. You will never know your purpose or place unless you seek Him for those answers. You cannot get them from others.

As a home builder, I often experience some pretty amusing things. (I could have said amazing instead of amusing.) I build custom homes, which involves my customers in the decision-making process of designing and building their homes. They tend to ask friends and relatives, or other acquaintances for their opinions. At times, this can be helpful. However, these people seldom know what this customer really wants, yet each has an opinion and is quite willing to offer it. I doubt you would ask an electrician about a plumbing decision if you had a plumbing decision to make. Nor would you ask a plumber about a decorating decision. While he or she may have some helpful ideas, they do not really know what you want and/or need. In other words, that is not their expertise!

In the same way, many of us go through life trying to discover our purpose in all kinds of ways. We go to school and ask teachers. We go to church and look for answers. We go to work and try to find the answer there. Sometimes, we marry, and hope our spouse will help us answer the question of *"What am I here for?"*

Many books have been written on this subject, some with good information. However, the bottom line is that you cannot find the answer from your teacher, coworker, boss, friend, pastor, priest, spouse, or from any book. You must get that information from the One who created you, and it only comes through relationship with Him. Think about it. Would you really want to rely on a plumber's advice to decorate your home? Thank God for plumbers, but I think I'll leave the plumbing to plumbers. Thank God for electricians, but I'll leave the electrical work to electricians.

My point is to put your trust in the only one who knows you, in this case, your Creator. He has gifted you uniquely, and knows you better than your spouse, your friends, your children, your pastor or priest, and even better the you yourself. That's right, He knows you better than you know yourself, which is exactly why you need to develop your relationship with Him. He, and He alone, knows what He created you for and can show you how to do what He created you to do.

When you are doing what God has created you to do, blessings come, but even then, if you get the attitude, *"Okay, Father, I see. Now I know my purpose!"* get ready for trouble. Why? Because you're back to relying on your own knowledge. This is why we must *constantly* seek Him in everything, not just some things. You see, He alone is God, The Father. Even though you receive Him and His nature, you are not capable of fulfilling His purpose without seeking Him. This is why Paul said, "Pray without ceasing." Only God knows what He has for you, and what's around the corner. We cannot see around the corner. If we were where He is, and had His perspective from above all, we would see all, but we don't have His vantage point and we cannot see the future.

This brings me to the next point. To put it simply, you are not in charge. You may certainly make many decisions concerning your life, but there is One who has greater authority concerning your life. If He calls you and chooses you, you are His. When you belong to Him, He has the responsibility of taking care of you. You have a responsibility to do what He has called you to do. When *both* parties of a relationship are doing what they are responsible to do, life is good and works the way it is supposed to work!

You've probably heard the expression, "When the boss is away, the workers play." If the boss is not in charge, things don't work the way they are supposed to work. I witnessed a good illustration of this a few years ago when my wife and I and some friends went to dinner at a local steak house. After we arrived, we waited nearly 45 minutes to be seated. While we waited, I couldn't help but notice several empty tables where we or someone else could have been seated, but many of them were not cleaned. Furthermore, no one seemed to be concerned about cleaning them with any sense of urgency but were instead ignoring them. There were several waiters, waitresses, hosts, and hostesses who were not busy. My parents had owned a few restaurants over the years, and having worked in them, I always pay attention to these details. I wanted to shout some orders, like *"Pick up a rag and buss tub and clean a table! You have many people here waiting for a table who would rather be seated than watching you visit while there are tables are just waiting to be cleaned!"*

I had wondered where the manager was, but I soon found out. He was in the kitchen, cooking. Evidently his main cook had not shown up or walked out. Whatever the reason, the boss (the manager) was not doing what he was supposed to be doing. To compensate for the slow kitchen, the wait staff deliberately delayed seating to slow down the orders to the kitchen. It was a disaster at that restaurant that evening because neither the boss nor the employees were doing what they were supposed to be doing.

Maybe your life is not what you would call a disaster or chaotic. (Or, maybe you have just decided chaos is normal!) Maybe life seems to be rolling along pretty smoothly. You may look around and see others' lives who seem to be in worse shape than yours, but the truth is that whether your life looks like a disaster, or whether it appears to be a success, it is not what it is supposed to be without a relationship between you and your Creator. I'm referring to a relationship in which both of you are doing what you are supposed to be doing. God will do His part because He is faithful. He is also the One in authority and His desire is for us to submit to His authority, because, after all, He knows what's best for us better than we do.

This is evident in what He has already done in our lives even before we knew Him. I encourage you to spend some time reflecting on your past. If you do, you will realize that all along He has been at work in your life, even though you may not have taken the time to notice.

Our Father knows His children and He desires to be known by them. Why is this? I've written much about the fact that God alone knows what's best for us because He created us, but why would God, the Creator of the universe, want to know *us? Furthermore, why would He care if we know Him?* I can only tell you, based on my personal experience, that it is simply a four-letter word: LOVE. I have experienced His love and am experiencing it daily. God's own words, written in 1 John 4:8, say, *"For he who does not love does not know God, for God is love."* God is love and it is love that motivates Him to desire an intimate, two-way relationship with us, where He knows us, and we know Him.

So, what you might ask, what is love? You just read it. God is love. I hope you will take some time to think on the principles shared in this chapter and reflect on how to apply them to your life. I wish I could hear all your thoughts right now, so I could personally respond to them. That would be ideal, but your thoughts are God's business. He does know your thoughts and the questions in your heart. Maybe that is why He told me to write about Him, and His love, because He knew you would be reading this today. I trust that as you read further, He will answer your questions.

Chapter Two

Fathers Pass on Wisdom to Their Children (Provision)

M ost of us are familiar with the phrases, *"Do as I say, not as I do,"* or *"Do it, because I said so."* As children, we may have heard them from our parents; as adults, we may have said them to our own children. If so, you probably meant well, but, in my experience, this approach simply does not work. I always needed to see things for myself, to experience things for myself. I was not very good at receiving instructions from others, even my own father. To put it mildly, I was a bit rebellious.

Like those who grow up in the "show me" state of Missouri, I never seemed to accept what someone else said. I wanted hands-on proof, or at least a demonstration, like "show and tell" in grade school. The expression "a picture says a thousand words" is true. There's merit to the fact that a visual demonstration is very helpful.

In our society today, we seem to be influenced much more by what we see than what we hear. Take high definition TV, for example. I had heard about HDTV for a year or so before my wife was finally able to persuade me to check it out. Just a few days ago, we bought one. This morning, as I was writing this chapter, Gina came into the room and turned it on. A program about Hawaii was on and seeing the clarity of pictures on HDTV was truly incredible.

However, the benefits of visualization went even further this morning. The program about Hawaii featured a particular island with two distinctly different environments. On one part of the island I saw beautiful landscapes of very rare, lush, green tropical plants, ninety percent of which are found only on this particular island. It was a perfect picture of vibrant life, with gorgeous plants everywhere. The other side of this island painted an entirely different picture, one of desolation, destruction, waste, and death. Volcanoes, many still active, had spewed out fiery lava and destroyed everything in their paths. The commentator explained that this part of the island was lost forever. Having these vivid pictures to show the contrast between the two environments, good versus harmful, life versus death, made a lasting impression on me much more effectively than if I only had a verbal description.

As I reflected on all this, I was reminded of a couple of Bible scriptures which seem very appropriate here. Matthew 5:19, 20, says, "Whoever therefore breaks one of the least of these commandments, and teaches men so, shall be called least in the kingdom of heaven; but whoever does and teaches them, he shall be called great in the kingdom of heaven. For I say to you, that unless your righteousness exceeds the righteousness of the scribes and Pharisees, you will by no means enter the kingdom of heaven."

Teaching His disciples here, Jesus is explaining that He came to fulfill the law, the commandments of God, not to destroy, but to fulfill. I see an important principle at work in this passage. People are taught good things by good actions and good examples, and/or bad things by poor actions and poor examples. *Actions speak louder than words.* Jesus not only taught with words, He lived out His teachings by example.

As a son, I learned both good and bad things by my father's example. Few things did I ever learn simply by words alone. As a father, I have also taught both good and bad things to my children by my example. Unfortunately, I've probably taught them more bad than good by my actions, which brings me to the second verse I was reminded of this morning. Proverbs 22:6 instructs us to "Train up a child in the way he should go, and when he is old, he will not depart from it." Notice this verse does not say *teach,* but *train.* To train is to show them a picture, to demonstrate, and better yet, to lead by example. So, we are to do both, *teach,* as the verse in Matthew instructs, and *train* as the verse in Proverbs instructs.

Both my father and my stepfather passed on wisdom to me in different ways. My father was only able to pass on to me wisdom from the world and his own environment, because that's all he knew. My stepfather, however, taught me some of the wisdom of the world, such as sound business principles, but he also taught me wisdom from the Bible, which is the word of God Himself.

A perfect picture of this in my life is something I learned from my stepfather when I was about nineteen or twenty. He shared with me that when he began to put action to the principles the Bible teaches about, he discovered things seemed to work out well. For example, he explained that he had begun tithing some years prior, as the Bible teaches. (Tithing simply means giving back to the Lord the first ten percent of everything one earns.) Although I did not immediately begin practicing tithing myself, I could certainly see the benefits of it in his life. I saw him practice what he taught, so I believed him. As I grew older, I began to tithe; eventually, as I was consistent, I, too, was blessed in everything I did. I believe that had he not practiced tithing himself, his words alone would not have persuaded me to do the same, but because I witnessed the principle operating in his life, I made the decision to do the same. As I did, it yielded blessings in my life, clearly a positive illustration of learning by teaching and training by example.

There were also many good things my natural father had taught me by example, such as a good work ethic. He faithfully got up every morning, went to work, and worked hard to provide for his family. He also showed me how to maintain the yard, the car, and our home. I'm grateful for the work ethic he instilled in me by example. Had he not shown me how to work and provide by his example, I may very well not have a good work ethic today.

Unfortunately, I also learned by his example, some harmful things. As a young boy, I remember wondering why he would say *not* to do something that he was doing himself. I thought, *"There must be a reason he's doing what he told me not to do. Is it because it's fun?"* I brilliantly concluded that it must be fun, so I decided to try "it." Consequently, I began smoking, drinking, driving too fast, using foul language, telling bad jokes, etc. Clearly, in these cases, my father's actions spoke louder to me than his words.

Many times he told me, *"Don't drink too much alcohol, it's dangerous!"* but the problem was he himself did drink too much. Over time, I followed his example rather than his words. Fortunately, for me, I later gave it up. However, he was not so fortunate. Eventually alcohol cost him his life, dying at the early age of forty-four. I was twenty-three at the time, old enough to realize what had caused his massive stroke. I later learned that his drinking had also contributed to his several failed marriages.

Both my father and my stepfather meant well in *instructing* me in the way I should go, the way I should live, but it was their actions that influenced me the most. The best way to pass on wisdom to our children is to not merely teach, but to train by example. In other words, *show and tell.* What a difference this one simple principle could make if parents, teachers, and employers would practice what they preach.

Is it any wonder that our children are confused by the many mixed messages they get from those of us who should know better? As fathers, it's so easy to leave it to mom or the teachers, or even just chance. Whether we fathers consider ourselves wise or not, we have a responsibility to pass on whatever wisdom we have gleaned in life. That instruction should be reflected in our behavior, not just because *"I said so."* We must realize, before it's too late, our children are influenced more by our actions than our words. Our words are powerful, but they carry more weight when backed up by actions that agree with our words. Words alone are usually ineffective. If we truly believe our words, our actions will show it.

I had friends and relatives whose fathers were better examples in that they did not drink, smoke, etc. Some of them followed their fathers' examples, never straying, while others did stray from the example of their fathers. You might wonder then, *why should I work so hard to be a role model if it doesn't guarantee my efforts will keep my children on the right path?* The answer is, if it keeps them from even some of the consequences of foolish choices and actions, it's worth it! Remember, the verse in Proverbs said, "When they are *old,* they will not depart from it." It did not say the child would *never* depart from it. Our children are influenced in many ways and by many people, like their friends, teachers, bosses, coaches, etc. In the end, however, none have more of an impact on us, whether positively or negatively, than our parents, particularly our fathers.

We're all familiar with the saying *you can lead a horse to water, but you can't make him drink,* often expressed when we observe a person not following what, they've been taught. Have you noticed this pithy saying does not say *tell* the horse (i.e., willful person) where the water is? It says to *lead* him to the water. Here again, when applying this to human behavior, we see the difference between teaching and training. Even so, the horse will still have the choice of whether to drink or not.

Likewise, as fathers, we must train and lead, but we cannot *force* our children to make the right choices. I know of many instances where a father or parent tried to force right choices on his or her child. Often, the child did just the opposite, just as a child who's been taught but not trained by example chooses to do. Human nature tends to innately view force as being unjust, oppressive, tyrannical. Consequently, even when force is intended to promote a good outcome, it may be counterproductive and drive a person away from the desired behavior.

Wisdom is not to be forced but introduced by example and demonstrated in love.

What does love have to do with the imparting of wisdom? Our children are much sharper than we often realize. They know when someone is not genuine or have their best interest at heart. Also, children know and will respond to love. You may be thinking, *Wait a minute! My children don't respond to the things I tell them to do, and I only do it out of love, because I truly care for them.* Remember, our Proverbs verse didn't promise children would follow now, but when they are old.

So, if you are wondering why your children aren't immediately accepting the wisdom you are trying to give them, ask yourself how long it took you to listen to the instruction of your parents. The waiting process may very well teach you patience, as you realize what your own parents might have experienced in raising you. By the way, how long did our Father God wait patiently for you to turn to Him?

The Bible tells a story of two sons, commonly referred to as the parable of the lost son, or the prodigal son. (Luke 15:11-32) The younger brother wanted his freedom to do his own thing, go his own way, so he asked his father for his inheritance. The scripture says, "So he gave to them his livelihood." In other words, he gave them all they needed for life, or equipped them for life. (Notice it says *them,* not just *him.*) So, the younger brother gathered his things and set out for a far away land. He was going to find his life! However, he ended up wasting his inheritance on foolish things, and fell on tough times. Destitute, he went to work for a pig farmer, feeding the pigs. He himself was starving and would gladly have eaten what he was feeding the pigs, but no one gave him anything. The Bible says he "came to himself" and remembered that even the hired hands of his father were well taken care of, had plenty to eat, and enjoyed a pretty good life, while here he was starving, and "perishing with hunger." He remembered the loving provision, the generosity his father had demonstrated by *example.*

So, he said, "I will arise and go to my father, and say to him, 'Father, I have sinned against heaven and before you, and I am no longer worthy to be called your son. Make me like one of your hired servants.'

"And he arose and came to his father. But when he was still a great way off, his father saw him and had compassion, and ran and hugged his neck and said to him, 'Father, I have sinned against heaven and in your sight, and am no longer worthy to be called your son."

Guess what the father did? He did not scold, reproach or treat his son as someone unworthy of his love; on the contrary, he threw a party and celebrated his son's return home! This father had obviously trained his son, prepared him for life, and the son did return home later, just as Proverbs 22:6 says.

And there's even more to be learned in this story. When we come to the end of the account, we find that the older brother, when he heard all the commotion from the party, came in from the field and asked one of the hired hands what all the commotion was about.

And he said to him, "Your brother has come, and because he has received him safe and sound, your father has killed the fatted calf." But he was angry and would not go in. Therefore, his father came out and pleaded with him. So, he answered and said to his father. "Lo, these many years I have been serving you; I never transgressed your commandment at any time' and yet you never gave me a young goat, that I might make merry with my friends. But as soon as this son of yours came, who has devoured your livelihood with harlots, you killed the fatted calf for him."

In essence, this older brother is saying, "I worked harder for you, stayed with you, and now I don't even get a goat burger, and he gets a rib eye! This isn't fair!" He's angry at his dad. He's been the good son. Shouldn't his father love him more? However, his father responded by saying, "Son, you are always with me, and all that I have is yours. It was right that we should make merry and be glad, for your brother was dead and is alive again, and was lost and is found."

The older brother who had served his father, and been an obedient son, didn't realize all that already belonged to him, not like his younger brother who had gone astray and then realized all that belonged to him. The older brother thought his dad loved them based on obedience, but clearly this story teaches us that the father's love was not based on how his children performed.

Many times, we don't appreciate what we have until we no longer have it. I see in this account that the father was happy not only because his son was safe, but because he was sound as well. The younger son returned home with a new perspective on life. Not only was he safe, but his thinking was straightened out. This is why the father said to the older brother, "Your brother was dead and is alive again, and was lost and is found."

Quite often, as our children get older, they grow apart from us as they seek to find their way in life. Nevertheless, if we have not merely taught them, but equipped them, training them as we should, and leading by example, we can expect that when they are older, they will not depart from our training. The younger son, while feeding pigs for someone who gave him nothing, remembered how his father not only provided for him, the son, but also provided well for his servants.

Remembering the picture of his father's love in action brought him back home. We, too, must paint our children a picture, not only with words of wisdom, but by our actions and the example we live before them.

Chapter Three

Fathers Have a Plan

I remember as a young boy looking forward to the chores my father had for me each day. That might seem strange to you if you're not a "type A" person like me. For me, I enjoy the sense of accomplishment that comes when I've finished my list.

A typical list for me in those days might have been: carry out the trash, shine dad's boots, clean my room, mow the lawn, edge the walks, rake leaves, help with the dishes after dinner, do some ironing, and perhaps even help with the cooking. My dad also had a plan for my brother, stepbrothers, sister, and mom, as well as himself.

As I grew older, I saw this concept applied in other areas of life. At school, the teacher had a lesson plan for each day, and the coach had practice plans for each day and a game plan for each game. When I began working, I had a plan after school, and sometimes on Saturdays, to mow yards, etc. When I went to work for an employer, he had plans as to how I was to do my job, plans for how much I would be paid if I did my job, and a plan to increase my pay as I improved and excelled in my work.

Eventually, I became an employer, and I created daily plans for my employees, as well as myself. Each night I would go to sleep, purposely thinking of the next day and what needed to be accomplished that day. I even dreamt about it while I slept. The next morning, when my employees showed up for work, I was ready to give them their instructions for the day. This system worked well for me. That way I stayed prepared to give my employees the directions and instructions they needed to complete our projects in a timely way.

Creating these plans taught me the value of purposeful thinking and specific planning, rather than just random, casual thought. I always disciplined myself to think about next steps.

When I later became a father, I began to think of and create plans for my children. I must admit they were often somewhat selfish, like taking the family on camping and fishing trips, because those were activities I happened to love. I'm not sure they enjoyed it as much as I did. Other times, I thought about making something for them or getting something, I knew they'd like, like a playhouse, or swing set, a tricycle or bicycle. At times, it was a ball and bat, or a basketball.

I sometimes wondered what they would become when they grew up. Would my girls be teachers, doctors, wives, detectives, tennis players, etc.? I paid attention to the things they liked to do and excelled at doing and wondered if those would be their direction in life. Over time, I usually discovered that what I thought they might do was not what they enjoyed doing when they grew up. As my children grew older, and were influenced by other people and things, their interests changed. Many times, the things they were so good at previously would no longer interest them, and yet I saw that those skills were still a help to them.

They were each unique in their ways and the rate in which they grew and changed. One would seem to "run wide open" all the time. Another would be more deliberate and slow to change. One would analyze every detail intellectually, and another would change course impulsively based on emotions and circumstances. One made friends easily, and another didn't seem to have many friends. One was caring and more of a follower, while another would take charge of every situation and jump in with both feet.

21

I remember watching their approach at a lake or swimming pool. One would cautiously put one toe in to test the water temperature. One would sit and watch what everyone else did first. Another would just dive in headfirst without thinking. Still another would wade in slowly. I have learned to appreciate the uniqueness of personality in each, while realizing that their pattern of behavior may change as they grow. The one who was most reverent and well behaved as a child may later turn out to be the most rebellious.

I've been told that as a young boy, I was a "good boy," and behaved pretty well. On the other hand, my younger brother was mischievous, and a little harder to handle. Later, our roles switched. As a teenager, I began to resist authority, and became the more rebellious of the two of us. My brother was involved in sports, and was much better at them than I was, which I believe helped keep him out of trouble somewhat. I, on the other hand, seemed to go looking for trouble. I am quite sure the thoughts and plans my parents had for us were not the way things turned out. Obviously, I cannot pretend to know their thoughts, but I do know as a father that our own thoughts and plans for our children are often not the way they turn out.

I'm reminded of a verse in the Bible that says this: "A man's heart plans his way, but the Lord directs his steps." (Proverbs 16:9) I've had many plans, dreams, expectations, desires, and wants in my life. Some have come to pass, most have not. Some came to pass and then I wondered, *"Why did I want this so much? It's not at all what I thought it would be."* Have you ever wondered why you wound up where you are? Have you ever wondered, *"What's missing? I thought this would be better than it is, this direction I've chosen, this career, this place I live, this marriage I've chosen."*

Another verse in the Bible speaks to these questions and thoughts. Proverbs 14:12 says, "There is a way that seems right to a man, but its end is the way of death." It seems to me the writer is talking about a path, or a road we can choose, a journey we can take in our lives, one that looks good to us. It may sound good, it might even taste good at first, but when we get there, it's nothing, it's empty. It has nothing more to offer - it's over.

I've not spent a lot of time thinking about death. Most people don't. It's not something we are comfortable with, and it just makes most of us uneasy to talk about it, so why think about it? Most of us have experienced death in some way. We may have lost someone close to us. We've felt a sense of finality and that thought is very hard to accept. The experiences we shared will not happen again, the things we took for granted are over, and cannot be shared anymore. It's a sudden reality of change in our lives and in the lives of others which we find very uncomfortable. So, if death is so empty, if it has nothing to offer, why would we deliberately take that path or choose that way? The verse says, "It seems right to a man." In other words, it seems right to us, in our own thinking. So, it becomes our plan, our way. I encourage you to take time to read the story of Adam and Eve's choice, found in Genesis, the first book of the Bible, chapters 2 and 3. You'll see that Adam and Eve chose a path that looked and seemed right to them.

After trying and working my plan, doing things my own way in life, I came to a place where life seemed very empty. I thought, *"Is this all there is? Is this it?"* I finally heard about and considered the fact that there must be a better way. I had heard about God several times as I was growing up. I believed He existed and that He probably created the world. In fact, I had once argued with my eighthgrade science teacher as he tried to teach us about creation with a big bang theory. I wasn't sure, but even then, I thought a person would have to be crazy to believe that all of this was the result of an explosion!

Finally, someone explained to me that I could have a relationship with the Creator of the universe. I heard that He, God Himself, had thoughts about *me* and *plans for me.* I was told God's thoughts were thoughts of good, not evil and they were to give me a future and a hope. I thought, *Ok, I'm in! The future and hope sounds good to me.* However, I was then told that I could not experience His plan for my life, that future and hope, because of sin in my life. He, the good and perfect God, could not dwell or hang out with sin. But then I heard that God the Father had a plan and a way for me to experience His good plans after all! His plan was to take care of that sin problem once for all people, not just for me, but for the whole world.

Fathers plan for their children; they have a plan and it's a good plan. I heard that God's plan, the Way, was through His Son Jesus, whom the Father sent to pay the penalty for our sins, the ways we all have chosen. I discovered that He died in our place on the cross for us, for me and you, so we would not have to die, so that we could come to the end of this life and not find emptiness and "nothing" forever, but that we could spend eternity with God, living as He is, forever alive.

I also was told that this is not something you can earn; you can't be good enough to deserve this on your own, according to your own ways. You must individually accept His free gift of His everlasting eternal love. I learned you must confess with your mouth and believe in your heart that the Lord Jesus died for you and that the Father raised Him from the dead and seated Him at His right hand. The day I heard these truths found in the Bible I was asked to pray with the gentleman who had explained them to me. He led me to pray, "Father, I accept your gift today. I confess that I've not been the person You created me to be. I've gone my own way but now I ask Your Son Jesus to come into my life today. I give Him control of my life to make me the person You created me to be. I believe that Jesus paid the penalty for my sins on the cross and that You raised Him from the dead to be my Lord and Savior. I need You to come into my life and be Lord of my life. Thank You for your gift. In Jesus' name, I pray.

Approximately thirteen years earlier, to the day, I had stood before a congregation and professed my faith in Him. I believe had I died during that time, I was saved, and probably would have gone to heaven to meet the One who created me. But I did not *know* Him. I only knew that He existed, and I hoped I would get to meet Him someday.

But thirteen years later, things were suddenly different. I'm not sure, but I believe it's because my heart was right this time. I didn't just believe with my mind, but with my heart. The Bible teaches us that man looks at the outside, but God knows the intents of our heart. You can't fool God. He knows exactly what you really desire. The Bible also teaches that He will give you the desires of your heart. Wow! What a gentleman! He knows what we truly want and that's what He gives us. He knows what we need, but He gives us what we desire.

I had been seeking to get to know Him for some time before I prayed that prayer. I was reading my Bible everyday and not just a couple of verses. I know now that God knew my heart's desire, and He also knew the plan He mapped out, and that my desire must be confessed with my mouth as well as believed in my heart, according to His plan, not mine.

Almost immediately, I noticed a real change in my attitude, particularly in my view of others, especially complete strangers. The old me would hardly notice others or a possible need they might have. I had been too wrapped up in myself and my own plans to even notice others. Oh sure, I would see them and maybe smile or open a door, or say, *"how're you doing?,"* like most decent people, but I didn't take time to notice if something was wrong, or if they were in need of something I could give them.

Now I was noticing others, and it was something new to me, something very fulfilling and satisfying to me. I found that I actually loved helping others! It was better than fishing, better than my job as a builder! I also began to realize that I hadn't loved my family the way God intended me to love them, constantly and consistently, just like He loves me. The same was true of my love for my friends - I hadn't loved consistently or constantly. I had based my love on their performance or their treatment of me, and my interests, rather than genuinely accepting them just as my Father had accepted me, simply because of His nature and who He is, rather than because of anything I had done.

However, the most rewarding thing of all was that as I sought Him, and His plan for my life, I developed a personal relationship with Him. I was not just praying a one-way prayer, hoping He heard it and might then put His stamp of approval on my plan. No, now I was actually asking Him what His plan was for me, and I was hearing it, little by little. Over time, our relationship has grown. I've discovered for myself the truth - He is God the Father and is a rewarder of those who diligently seek Him.

I've also discovered that His plan is far better than any of the ones I had tried. The prophet Isaiah reveals God's heart in Isaiah 55:9,10:

"For as the heavens are higher than the earth, so are My ways higher than your ways, and My thoughts than your thoughts. For as the rain comes down, and the snow from heaven, and do not return there, but water the earth, and make it bring forth and bud, that it may give seed to the sower and bread to the eater, so shall My word be that goes forth from My mouth. It shall not return to Me void, but it shall accomplish what I please, and it shall prosper in the thing for which I sent it."

26

This means that God has a better plan for my life than I do, and much of it is higher than I can understand at this time. For me to be writing this book is so much greater than the plans I had that it is hard to believe, but as He said, His ways are higher than mine. This therefore means that if I follow His plan instead of mine, it will work, and not fail. It will accomplish His will, exactly as He intends it to do. I have truly discovered the Father's plan, and it does prosper in the thing to which He sent it, just as the verse in Isaiah says.

Many who surrender to His plan assume they must give up everything and stop doing what they are currently doing. I, too, assumed that at first. I thought, *Well, I guess I wasn't intended to be a builder. Maybe I should become a pastor or an evangelist, like the ones who have inspired me.* However, I discovered that, for the time being, I didn't need to stop being a builder. His plan was not so much about changing what I did for a living but changing the way I view it and do it, my perspective on it. My new perspective according to my Father's plan is that I'm not providing for me and my family, but He, my Father, is my provider. It is He who gifted me with the talents I have, and His plan is for me to use those talents for His purposes.

In my business, I have many opportunities to build relationships. If I view my business as a means to get money and provide for my family, then those relationships won't be lasting or very meaningful, nor would I give them the service they deserve. However, if I know that God has purpose in them, then I know why I do it: it is for Him and His purposes. This takes the focus off of me and meeting my needs and places it on using my God-given talents to serve my customers in a way that pleases my Father. When I do that, He provides for my needs, and my customers get more than they expected. Likewise, if I view my employees as a means to meet my needs, this will also ruin any opportunity for building a meaningful and lasting relationship. But when I focus on serving a need for them, such as training and teaching them, providing for them first, that will produce a response of gratitude and a good working relationship.

This same principle holds true in our families. If we believe providing for our family's wellbeing only means earning a living, we will also ruin our opportunity for building meaningful and lasting relationships with them. In Ephesians 2:10, Paul writes to the church about the Father's plan: "For we are His workmanship created in Christ Jesus for good works, which God prepared beforehand that we should walk in them." We are to be doing good works for and to others. In chapter 4 of Ephesians Paul writes about unity in Christ - how we are to act and conduct ourselves in the church, the body of Christ, with humility, lowliness, gentleness and longsuffering toward others, bearing with one another in love. In chapters 5 and 6, Paul tells us to imitate our Father as dear children. He addresses family relationships with instructions for husbands, wives, fathers, and children. These instructions are our Father's plan, which gives us a different perspective than our own plan, and once again, His plan never fails. Following His plan yields lasting and meaningful relationships in which we share the love of the Father with each other.

When I draw plans for the homes I build, or an architect draws them, we draw different viewpoints of the details of the home in order to show the contractors how to build the home. This is what our Father has done in giving us His plans for life in Christ. He has given us a new perspective of the details of relationships in life: first with Him, and then with others, which can then become relationships that are meaningful, purposeful, and significant.

Chapter Four

Fathers Protect Their Children

A father's protection is not always received for what it is. Many times, protection comes in the form of discipline. We are often not comfortable with discipline, so we don't recognize it as something that is meant for our protection. Discipline is a good thing, not a bad thing.

As a child, I can remember thinking of discipline as a form of punishment. I didn't always realize it was actually good for me, that it was meant for my protection. Consequently, I believe the way discipline is perceived is as important as discipline itself. If I view discipline as punishment rather than protection, I'm not as likely to receive it. Therefore, I might be more likely to ignore the importance of the correction, correction that was actually intended for my protection.

For example, if I tell my child, *"Don't ride your bike on Main Street. If you do, I'll ground you."* He or she might still choose to do it because it's the faster way to their friend's house. Or, I could explain it a different way, like *"I don't want you to ride your bike on Main Street because it is very busy with traffic; people are just not watching out for bike riders the way they should. I don't want you to get hurt because I love you."* My child could still choose to ride on Main Street, but I believe they would be far less likely to do so, when I explain it in that manner.

Unfortunately, I seldom took the time to do that with my children, nor did my father with me. I've often wondered why that is, but I've never come up with an adequate excuse. However, I can think of many explanations, such as "I'm too busy," "I didn't have time," "Why don't they just do what I say? Why do they need to know why?"

I remember a time in my early twenties, when I had an old 1950 Chevy pickup truck. I was taking the transmission out in my driveway. My neighbors, in their sixties at that time, had a three or four year old granddaughter, and she was fascinated with my work. She would crawl down next to me and watch. If I was loosening a bolt, she would say, *"John, what ya doing that for?"* I would say something like, *"So I can get this transmission out."* She would respond with *"Why?"* or *"What for?"* I would answer and again she would repeat her question, *"Why?"* We spent many days going back and forth like that. Looking back, and reflecting on that, I realized something about children: They want to know things. They are curious by nature, hungry for the truth about everything.

That was a much simpler time in my life. I didn't have much, wasn't nearly as busy as I am now, didn't know as much as I do now, and the truth is, I wasn't as distracted by all the responsibilities and possessions I've now acquired. The more I get, the more time it takes to care for it. The bigger the yard, the more yard work it takes, and therefore the more time it takes to care for it. We want nice things for our children, so we work harder and harder to buy them more. Then before we know it, our children are grown, moving out on their own, going off to school, and finding their careers. I find myself asking *"why didn't I spend more time with them, while I had a chance? I had so much more to say, to give, and to explain."*

Actually, that's not true. The truth is, I did not have that much more to say, to give, or to explain. The fact is, I was not prepared to be the father I should have been. The things I could have shared with them were not the kind of wisdom they needed.

I had more foolishness to give than wisdom, and foolishness is not likely to protect anything worth protecting. A father can only give what he has, and unfortunately, I didn't have much. I was too busy worrying about me. That's right, me! *"What do I want to do today?" Go fishing, hunting, hang out with friends, clean the garage, work on the yard, wash the truck, paint the house?"*
You get the idea. It's something we all deal with. It's called selfishness. My world centered on me. I was the center of my world. Every thought went through the filter of "me-first." If there was something left, maybe I could give up some of the leftovers. That's the way I lived: me, myself, and I first. After all, if I didn't look after me, who would? I was taught to fend for myself. After all, isn't that what men are supposed to do? They grow up, become a man, and provide for themselves and their family.
There are a couple of problems with this, plan, the first being there's no time left after worrying about myself, let alone after worrying about my family, too. Worrying takes a lot of time, and it is absolutely a total waste of time. Secondly, it's like trying to drive up a steep and long hill or mountain in reverse, going backwards down the hill as fast as you can. In other words, you're not only going the wrong way, but you are gaining speed by going downhill instead of uphill. It's the exact opposite of what you need to do to get where you want to go. Worrying will change nothing except steal from the time you have to get to your destination.
So, since the main issue seems to be "me first," how do I overcome it? Obviously, I've been spending so much time worrying about me, and my agenda, that I've little or no time left for my family and others. My own answer came when I found a truth in the Bible, Matthew 6:33: "But seek first the kingdom of God and His righteousness, and all these things shall be added to you." Jesus was teaching on the subject of worrying about

your life, things like your body, what to wear, drink, or eat. He said that life is more than these, and not only that, "look at the birds of the air. They neither sow nor reap nor gather into barns." In other words, they are not worrying about all those things, "yet your Heavenly Father feeds them. Are you not of more value than them?" He's telling us to stop worrying about ourselves, that's His job. He's saying, "I'm supposed to take care of you, and I do, so stop it. Here's what I want you to do: **seek Me first** and my way of doing things, and I'll take care of you and your stuff." Evidently, It's God's place to protect and provide for me. If I understand that, maybe it would free me to care for others, both my family and others.

So, how do I seek Him first? It starts with a choice, a decision to trust Him with my life. If we look at the birds, as He said, they don't spend any time worrying about their care. They just sing and make beautiful sounds, fly freely through the air. They know somehow their provision will be there when they need it, as it always has been. Likewise, we must trust and believe that God will continue to do what He has done. If we can really trust Him with our care, then maybe we can protect and provide for our children, just as the birds take what the Lord has provided them, and give it to their young, until it is time to push them out of the nest.

The problem with many of us is that we spend most of our lives doing the opposite. We spend all of our time worrying about ourselves and our stuff. Then, maybe after we acquire some of that stuff, we begin to look toward God. We ask, *"Isn't there something more than this? Isn't life more than this?"* The answer, of course, is yes, just as Jesus said in Matthew 6:25, *"Is not life more than food and the body more than clothing?"*

So, what is life, if it is more than just us, and stuff for us? Jesus says in John 10:10, "The thief does not come except to steal, and to kill, and to destroy; I have come that they may have life and that they may have it more abundantly." He explains in the very next verse, "I am the good shepherd. The good shepherd gives His life for the sheep." So, Jesus gave His life in order that we could have a more abundant life. One translation says, to "have and enjoy life," not only that we could have eternal life, but to enjoy it. The thief (the devil) wants to steal, kill, and destroy life from you. If you're like me, the devil has stolen a lot.

Maybe you're thinking, *"How could the devil steal life from you?"* If I were to write all the examples in my life alone, it would be enough to write another book. However, let me share just a few ways he worked to kill, steal, and destroy my life.

I'll start with the killing first. When I was just two, my mother and father had their third child, my sister. She only lived three days. I believe this caused my parents' marriage to fail. They quickly grew apart and divorced. This resulted in my brother and me going to live with our grandparents while my parents tried to find a way to start over in their lives, careers, and new relationships. The thief (the devil) destroyed their relationship. At this same time, he stole our parents from us.

This started a cycle in my family. The Bible calls this a familiar spirit. We used to call it "monkey see, monkey do." You know, follow what you see, patterns you're familiar with. My father, I'm sure in trying to heal his wounds of losing his child, began drinking more, probably a lot more. Mom probably wanted to deal with the loss much differently, maybe by talking about it, trying to get an answer to what had gone wrong. They grew apart instead of together. So, they got a divorce and started over, separately. They each married a new spouse and started a new family. Dad married five more times to four different women, one of them twice. Mom married two more times. Both struggled with relationships because of a deep hurt from the loss of their child.

33

Years later, the cycle repeated. I, like my father, got married pretty young and started a family. We lost our second child, Jamie. When I went to pick her up at the babysitter's one day after work, we went to get her from the bed where she was sleeping. She was blue, and not breathing. We called for an ambulance, but she did not make it. Later, they told us this was SIDS - Sudden Infant Death Syndrome. Doctors don't know why, but a child just stops breathing, which in turn, causes the heart to stop. Then, just as my parents had done, my wife and I each dealt with our pain differently. We didn't talk about it with each other. I just drank more and more to try to forget it. I didn't want to talk about it with anyone. We had twins soon thereafter, which certainly helped, and later had our fifth daughter. But we, just like my parents, grew apart.

There are many similar things that get passed on from generation to generation. Alcoholism is only one. It might be some other type of addiction or dependency. It may be a type of insecurity, such as lack of self- confidence. It could be a mean spirit, or a pattern of arrogance or pride. There are far too many to name them all, but the question is, *"How do fathers protect or guard their families from these cycles of destruction?"*

First, we have to recognize there is a problem: Are there things, not right? Things that seem to be a pattern in your family that reoccur in each generation, something that steals, kills, or destroy relationships? Maybe you've noticed that problems your parents or grandparents had are showing up in your life. As I think back to when I was between five and eight years old, during the time I stayed with my grandparents, I saw my grandmother sneak drinks of something during the day. Many times, by the end of the day, she would curse my grandfather, usually from the next room, behind the doorway. I didn't realize until much later that my own father must have witnessed this much of his life as a child, as well.

After my father passed away, at only forty-four, I thought, *"I'm not going to drink as much as he did."* I was twenty-three at the time, and drinking some, mostly beer, but occasionally something stronger. I decided then that I would not let this happen to me. I was only half right, because even though I pretty much avoided the strong stuff, I still drank too much, and it eventually played a big part in my divorce. I knew my father had a problem, but I was unwilling to recognize my own problem. I thought I was ok and wasn't as bad as others because I could stop drinking before I was too drunk, and I didn't lose control completely. Wrong! A problem, whether big or small, is still a problem.

The Bible teaches something we might interpret as radical amputation. Matthew 5:29 says, "If your right eye causes you to sin, pluck it out and cast it from you; for it is more profitable for you that one of your members perish, than for your whole body to be cast into hell." In other words, get rid of the problem, get away from it, separate yourself from it. I tried to put a bandage on it, to fix it instead of getting rid of it. Unfortunately, I didn't get rid of it until after I had passed it on to my children. I don't think any of them have developed a serious problem with it yet, and I pray they will not before they get rid of it.

We tend to think that if our "problem" is held in check, it's not a problem. We don't realize that it changes the way we think, even if we don't drink much. So, when I recognize that something may be a problem, whatever the problem may be, I need to get rid of it, just quit doing it. Sounds simple enough, however, many of us may need help. How does a father protect his children from these problems? Earlier, we established that he needs to be the example. Our children need a picture; unfortunately, many of us have failed to paint a good picture for our children.

As I've thought about my life and the many narrow escapes I've experienced, I can think of several ways that both my natural fathers and my Father God have protected me. My natural father provided correction throughout my life, often by speaking things to me, sometimes very specific things, and at other times with pithy sayings that might seem funny, but which gave advice. One of these he used to say often was "If you mess with the bull, you'll get the horns," a warning but with humor. Because we laugh at this type of saying, we tend to not take them too seriously. So, while they actually contain truth, they are probably not the most effective way to protect your children. Sayings like these, pale in comparison to just spending time with our children explaining sound principles of wisdom and setting boundaries for them.

Wisdom is the ability to live life skillfully. Fathers get wisdom from their fathers and from experiences in their lives and from others who have influenced them. Unfortunately, the wisdom we receive often gets watered down or muddied by many other influences. Perhaps your father gave you some advice or wisdom and then someone else, like a friend, or a teacher, an employer, or even your mom, said something along the same lines, but a little bit different. Now the wisdom has another twist, and the waters are muddied.

Also, we sometimes allow our circumstances and emotions to distort wisdom. We attach the "buts" to it. For example, Dad said to put ten percent of my allowance back for later, when I may need it. But my friend or someone else says "if you want that candy now, you'll need that ten percent." So, I allow the waters of wisdom to be muddied. Or, I may have a friend who is doing something wrong, and I know it. I ask my Dad what to do about it. He says to go to them and tell them the truth about what they're doing and the consequences they face. So, all I need to do is just go to them and spit it out, right? But on the way to my friend, I start hearing the "buts" in my mind: "But I don't want my friend to be mad at me! What if he gets mad at me and I lose my friend?" Or my emotions kick in, "I don't feel like doing this; it doesn't feel right."

By yielding to these three things I call the "buts" - listening to others, circumstances, and emotions - I've let wisdom become distorted. This is exactly how we've become unwilling to accept any absolute truths, both in our personal lives as well in the ways of the world. This is why we have so many complex laws in our country. It seems we must have one for every circumstance and every emotion and we must consider everyone's opinion. I expect we will continue writing them as long as we have new circumstances, emotions, and opinions.

So, as fathers, how do we protect our children with wisdom? Over the past several years, I have spent a lot of time reading the many great stories of the Bible. I am convinced there is a story for every circumstance and every emotion we may ever face. If I know there is help for each of these circumstances and emotions in the Bible, perhaps all I need to do is point my children to the Bible and let them find out for themselves. This is true, but there's more to it than that.

You see, the stories in the Bible are all about the love of God the Father has shown toward His children, each one motivated by love because that's who God is. So, the short answer is that we must first love our children because until they know how much we love them, they will not believe that what we are telling them is good for them. They will believe our correction is motivated simply to punish them. Or, they'll think we just want them to do right in order for us to be proud of them. They need to know that we are motivated to protect them out of a genuine love for them. Once they realize that, they will accept the advice or correction, and it will protect them from making foolish decisions that ultimately could cause them harm. When love is received, it will produce the same: a response of love. But it must first be sown as a seed. You plant it, continue to add to it by watering and feeding it, it grows and eventually it produces its fruit - love returned.

A simple story I heard in a men's group illustrates this very well. A young teenage girl was visiting with a group of her school friends one evening, when one of them suggested they do something that her father had taught her she should not do. She quickly spoke up and said, "No, I'm not going to do that." Her friends responded by saying, "Oh, you're just afraid you'll get caught, aren't you?" She replied, "No, I just don't want to hurt my father." This is a response of love. It is also a child honoring her father, just as the Bible instructs children to do. Proverbs 23:15,16 says; "My son, if your heart is wise, My heart will rejoice indeed, I myself; Yes, my inmost being will rejoice when your lips speak right things." I'm certain if the father of the young girl had been able to hear her words to those trying to convince her to do something wrong, his heart would have rejoiced. Being a father, I can imagine, how he would well up with pride for his daughter and say, "That's my girl!"

However, even as good as it feels, we must guard against desiring love and affection more than the truth. What do I mean? I mean that all too often we fathers, so desire that our children love us, that we get confused. We think they must like everything we say, believing that if they are just happy, they will love us. Wrong! Happiness is not just an emotion any more than love is not just an emotion. It is a choice!

As fathers, we have to guard our children in order to protect them. Love is the answer, but we must understand love. A father's love is a love that will tell the truth in every situation, not give the child everything he or she wants to hear or desires. It's a trap to think we have to keep them happy all the time, make them happy with every decision we make concerning them. By doing that we are caving into them and letting them do things and go places we know we should not allow, all because we are afraid they won't love us if we are too strict. The truth is we must protect them from themselves and the corruption that is out there in their path.

Another Bible story, found in the first and second chapters of I Samuel, tells about a priest named Eli and his two sons, Hophni and Phinehas, who both served in the temple. When people would bring their yearly sacrifice to the temple as an offering to the Lord, Hophni and Phinehas would keep it for themselves. It was customary for them to keep a portion of it, but these two kept all of it and threatened those who brought the meat offering that if they didn't offer it, it would be taken by force from them. This caused the people to hate the offering to the Lord. They also would lie with women who came to bring offerings. Hophni and Phinehas's sins were great before the Lord.

Eli knew what his sons were doing because he would hear about it from the people. He spoke to his sons, saying, "Why do you do such things? For I hear of your evil dealings from all the people. No, my sons! For it is not a good report. I hear you make the Lord's people transgress." The Lord spoke to Eli and told him he had honored his sons more than he honored the Lord and told him it would cost him his sons. This may sound harsh to you, but it teaches us an extremely important point about why we must love our children enough to correct them. It is true that the Lord took these two sons from Eli. He had even allowed Eli to become a priest, but what caused the Lord to take the two sons? It was a father's love, the *Father's love.*

The Lord loves His people so much He must protect them from sin, so when Eli's two sons caused people to sin, God, the Father, stepped in and took out the two sons. Had Eli corrected his sons with more than simply a few words, and followed the correction with discipline, exercising his authority and removing them, the two sons might have been saved. However, Eli did not do that. Like many of us, he chose the easy way out, and said, "I'll just speak to them and let them make their own decision."

I realize this goes against everything we hear in the world today, but truth trumps all the teachings of men. I did not write this story in the Bible, but I accept is as truth. It is the Word of God. It is the Word of God the Father and it must be honored more than our feelings, emotions, circumstances, and current trends of the world. If not, we may suffer the consequences. It is not enough for us to sit by and watch our children fall just because we fell, or the world says they have to learn it for themselves. We must discipline them according to the truth by speaking the truth to them and by exercising the authority given to us as fathers to enforce the truth. We must set boundaries and enforce them. Without consequences for their actions, the truth will not be revealed. If only words of instruction are given to our children, all we can do is say "I told you so." No one likes to hear "I told you so." When consequences are in place and enforced, the truth is revealed.

For example, if Eli had chosen to set boundaries and enforced them, he would have removed his sons from their positions and separated them from him. Although they might have perceived it as punishment, it would have protected them from themselves and their sin and ultimately might have saved them. This is what God the Father did by removing them. He protected His children from harm by removing those who caused harm to them. It was motivated by love, not anger. We must do the same as fathers. We must act to remove our children from harm's way.

It is not enough to live a life that is a good example and speak right words to our children. After all, Eli was a priest, a man of God, but he lost his sons - not because it was God's will - but because he failed to enforce and protect truth in their lives. Instead of leaving it to chance or someone else, we must take a stand for the truth. The truth is established in God's Word. It is the only absolute truth we have. Many do not believe that absolute truth exists. It is obvious to me that today many are living and raising their children as if there are no absolute truths. Someone once said, "If you don't believe in something, you will fall for anything." The "something" we need to believe in is the Word of God. It is the only absolute truth that has stood unchanged and unwavering from the beginning. God reveals truth to us and puts His Spirit in us to guide us in the way we should live and to protect us from the evils of this world.

How can we get our children to believe in the truth revealed in the Word of God? The Bible teaches in Romans 10:17, "So then faith comes by hearing, and hearing by the Word of God." Our children must hear the Word of God. It's not hard for us to share with them the wisdom we've learned in the world, the things we learned from men in school, in business and in our experiences, but when it comes to what God has done for us, sometimes we shy away. Psalms 107:21,22 says "Oh that men would give thanks to the Lord for His goodness, and for His wonderful works to the children of men! Let them sacrifice the sacrifices of thanksgiving and declare His works with rejoicing." The writer is referring to God's people who had many times seen and experienced the goodness of God in business and in the things of life. They had done many foolish things, following their own ways, and refusing to hear the voice of God. They would get into grave situations and distresses, and then cry out to the Lord for help. Verse 20, the preceding verse, tells us "He sent His word and healed them, and delivered them from <u>their destructions</u>." In other words, He protected them from <u>themselves</u> and the messes <u>they created</u> and <u>got themselves into</u>. But they refused to remember all the times He delivered them out of <u>their troubles</u>. Instead, they took their deliverance for granted, not offering any thanksgiving nor telling others of the great and wonderful things the Lord had done for them.

We should always be thanking God continually for all His good and wonderful works. It is He that gives us life, our skills, our talents, the ability to get wealth, our children, and our spouses. Everything that is good in life comes from Him! That is certainly worth a simple sacrifice of thanksgiving. After all, most of us wouldn't hesitate to thank someone for something as simple as holding a door open for us. But that verse in Proverbs didn't stop there. It said, "Declare His works (not ours) with rejoicing." We ought to be excited to tell others about the incredible things He has done for us. We should especially tell our children!

I'm reminded of a major miracle that God recently performed which made worldwide news. A plane had just taken off from the airport when it evidently met with a flock of geese. One of them was sucked into one of the engines. The pilot was able to land the plane in the Hudson River and all the crew and passengers were rescued. I've heard a few interviews with the pilot, certainly not all of them, but I've yet to hear anyone talk about God's divine intervention. It's a pattern that continues to be reflected throughout history: we tend to look at the greatness of men rather than to give credit to Whom it is due. We fail to give thanks to God for the Works He does to the children of men. Seven times in Psalm 107, we are instructed to give thanks to God for His works and His deeds.

One of the best ways to declare His works is to share with others what He has done in our own lives. Proverbs 20:6 says, "most men will proclaim each his own goodness, but who can find a faithful man?" We spend more time talking to our children about what we have done than what God has done for us and in us. Paul writes in Romans 10:14, "How then shall they call on

Him in whom they have not believed? And how shall they believe in Him of whom they have not heard? And how shall they hear without a preacher?" A preacher is one who tells about good things, good news. He is not one who constantly complains about what's going on and all the troubles he is having. He is one who has experienced the goodness of God and talks about that, about all the good things the Lord has done in his life. Therefore, I believe it is a father's responsibility to share the goodness of God with his children, assuming of course that the father has realized the goodness of God. To talk about God rather than ourselves requires humility, not just overcoming pride in ourselves, but actually getting ourselves out of the way so God can work through us.

We tend to misunderstand true humility. We think it's what we see in men who are willing to yield to another man, which is a good thing in most cases. However, humility before God is not before men. In the story of Job, we can see that his confidence was in God. He feared Him and shunned evil, the scriptures say. Job was such an upright man that God knew Satan could not tempt him into cursing God. Job was one who was truly blessed. He had everything until Satan began to steal from him. He believed God and trusted Him, but something happened when he lost everything. He didn't stop loving and trusting in God, but he began to question and reason as to why such things would happen to him. After all, he hadn't sinned as far as he could see.

I experienced something remotely similar a few years ago. Those who know me have heard me talk about what I call my "Job moment." One day while mowing the yard of a home I had for sale, I began complaining and whining about my circumstances. I was tired both physically and emotionally. I had two homes for sale at the time to mow as well as our own home. I was mowing them all with an inexpensive small push mower and spending lots of time sitting at them on weekends trying to sell them. I had built these two homes to sell - it's called speculative building, "specs" for short. I was never a big builder in terms of quantity, but I would build a couple every two years or so in order to attract more business. I had built these in two new areas, one a lake community and the other a small community where I had never built before. I wasn't getting much traffic at either home, and the stress, work, interest and maintenance were starting to wear on me. I began to complain to God and ask what was going on. I thought, *I read my Bible every day, I go to church every Sunday and Wednesday, I pay my tithes faithfully, I say my prayers every day. Why can't I sell these homes? Why am I not doing better? Don't I deserve better than this? Then it happened. I heard, "What are you supposed to be doing now?" I thought, Oh! I'm supposed to be thanking You and praising You for Your goodness.*

I immediately shut off the mower and began thanking God that I had the ability to mow three yards with that mower, that I even had a mower and a yard. Then I heard, "Did you ask Me about building those specs?" I responded, "No, Sir, I did not." *I realized I was complaining to God about a mess that I had created.*

So, I realized that day that I was trying to do God's part instead of my part, meaning I realized that I hadn't sought my Father's advice and direction for my family's provision. I was just doing what I thought was right. I knew my Father wanted to provide for me, but I hadn't asked Him to do that. I hadn't humbled myself before Him. Instead, I had trusted in my own righteousness. I was capable; my confidence was in myself, not in Him. I was seeking my own glory, not His. I remembered my favorite verse once again, Matthew 6:33, "But seek first the kingdom of God and His righteousness, and all these things shall be added to you." Verse 34 says, "Therefore, don't worry about tomorrow for tomorrow will worry about its own things.

Sufficient for the day is its own trouble." I realized that it is God's desire to provide for me and His ways are far better than mine. As the scriptures say, His ways are higher than ours. My job is to trust Him and to seek His righteousness, His ways, not just for my own personal benefit but because He is God and His ways are higher than mine. Regardless of my circumstances, He is still God. He has not changed, and He has not left me. I was the one who had chosen to go it alone.

I went home that afternoon a changed man. I told my wife we didn't need to worry any more. She probably thought I was crazy, but within a couple of weeks, we began to see real change in our circumstances, and we got contracts on our homes. Eventually, as we trusted in God for our needs instead of trusting ourselves, He led us away from the speculative market. He has blessed us with custom homes to build, remodels, and commercial projects ever since that day.

You may be wondering how this compares to Job? Here's how I understand it: The Bible says Job was a blameless man, upright and one who feared God and shunned evil. (Job 1:1) He was wealthy in every respect: a big family, lots of livestock, servants, and many possessions. In fact, the Bible describes him as the greatest of all the people of the East. He made daily sacrifices for his sons to cover their sins. You may know the story: God allowed Satan to attack Job and told Satan that Job was one who feared God and shunned evil. Satan responded by asking God, "does Job fear God for nothing?" Basically, Satan was saying, *No wonder Job fears you, look at all he has! But if You take away all that he has, he will surely curse You."* Then God told Satan, "You do it. I'll give you power over everything he has, but do not lay a hand on his person." So, Satan began to steal all the Job had. However, it was as God had said, Job would not quit fearing Him.

Once again God and Satan talked. God told Satan, "Have you noticed, in spite of all you have taken from him, he still holds fast to his integrity, even though you incited Me against him to destroy him without cause?" Satan responded, "Stretch Your hand against his flesh and bone and he will surely curse You to Your face." God replied, "Behold, he is in your hand, but spare his life." So, Satan struck Job's health severely with boils from head to toe so that even his own wife told him to "curse God and die." But in all this Job did not sin with his mouth. Then his three friends came and sat with him for seven days and nights. No one spoke a word to him, for they saw his grief was great. After this, Job opened his mouth and began complaining (just as I did in that yard). He cursed the day he was born and wondered why he hadn't died at birth. He said, "The thing I greatly feared has come upon me, and what I dreaded has happened to me. I am not at ease, nor am I quiet; I have no rest, for trouble comes." The Bible teaches that as a man thinks in his heart, so is he, and out of the abundance of the heart, the mouth speaks.

Then, one of Job's friends came to him and accused him of sin. He told him he had a word come to him in the night during which, fear and trembling came upon him. He heard a voice say, "Can a mortal become more righteous than God?" We can get a clue that this voice was not from God because God always tells us to "fear not." God does not operate that way. God always operates in love, not fear. Then God began to correct Job and to chasten him. He said to him, "Affliction does not come from the dust nor does trouble spring from the ground; man is born to trouble as the sparks fly upward. But as for me, I would seek God, and to God I would commit my cause, Who, does great things and unsearchable, marvelous things without number." He goes on to say, "Behold, happy is the man whom God corrects; therefore, do not despise the chastening of the Almighty. He bruises, but He builds up; He wounds, but His hands make whole. You shall be hidden from the scourge of the tongue, and you shall not be afraid of destruction when it comes. You shall laugh at destruction and famine and you shall not be afraid of the beast of the earth. For you shall have a covenant with the stones of the field, and the beasts of the field shall be at peace with you. You shall know that your tent is in peace; you shall know that your descendants shall be many, and your offspring like the grass of the earth. You shall come to the grave at a full age, as a sheaf of grain ripens in its season. Behold this we have searched out; it is true, hear it, and know for yourself."

What has God just said to Job? He said, you need to seek Me. This is good for you. It will make you happy. You won't be afraid. Every step you take will be secure; you'll walk on rocks and you won't stumble; you won't be afraid of the unknown or the beast. You will have peace in your heart when you know, but you must know it for yourself.

Job couldn't see any good coming from this. He felt he didn't deserve this destruction. His strength was gone, and he felt he could endure it. I felt those same emotions and pain, even though I'm sure my pain was not as great as what Job endured. The problem was that Job and I were both looking at our own abilities, and our own uprightness. We didn't understand that God was doing something for us and for Him. We did not realize that God is God. He and His will are much greater than our own will. Life is not about us it is about Him. When we fear for ourselves and our own wellbeing, we are no good to anyone. We lose our ability to hear from God the direction that we need for His works and His plans for our lives. When we begin to trust in our own abilities and works, we are not living the life that God created for us.

Imagine being in a game - football, basketball, baseball, soccer, any competitive sport - and getting your plays from the opposing coach. That's the way most of us live, getting our plays from the opposing coaches - ourselves! God the Father protects His children from themselves, and we as fathers must do the same for our children.

In Job's defense, he did not have the written word of God to refer to. Scholars believe that Job is perhaps the oldest book of the Bible. However, I unlike Job, *did* have God's Word to read and meditate on. This helped me to recognize what I was doing wrong when I heard clearly the instruction, "You are not supposed to be complaining, you are supposed to be praising God." So, I began thanking Him and praising Him, and not long after that, I had a knowing for myself from God Himself. I knew that He had a covenant with me. He was going to continue to provide for me, just as He always had, even when I did not know it.

The book of Job continues for several chapters with Job debating and pleading his case, never cursing God, just questioning his affliction and problems. His three friends were convinced Job's afflictions were because of some hidden sin in his life. But God said they too were wrong in their thinking. Then entered Elihu, a young man stirred up with anger against Job because he justified himself rather than God. Elihu was also angry with Job's friends who could not give Job an answer, yet they condemned him. He said, "I might be young but great men are not always wise, but there is a spirit in a man, and the breath of the Almighty gives him understanding." He explained that the spirit (not his mind) within him compelled him to speak: "I must open my lips and answer." He prayed, "Let me not show partiality to anyone; nor let me flatter any man. For I do not know how to flatter, else my Maker would soon take me away. My words come from my upright heart (not his head). God is greater than many, why do you contend with him? He does not give an accounting of His words. He might speak in one way or another, but man does not understand it."

Elihu explained that God opens the ears of men and seals their instruction. In order to turn man from his deed (his own plan) and conceal pride from man, God keeps back his soul and his life from perishing. If there is a messenger for him, a mediator, one among a thousand to show man God's uprightness, then He, God, is gracious to him, and says, "Deliver him from going down to the Pit. I have found a ransom; his flesh shall be young like a child's he shall return to the days of his youth. He shall pray to God, and He will delight in him; he shall see His face with joy, for He restores to man His righteousness." Then he looks at men and tells them, "I have sinned and perverted what was right, and it was not good for me.' And then God will redeem his soul from dying and his life will see light. Pay attention: God does all these things. Listen to me and I will teach you wisdom." Elihu continues to tell Job about the goodness of God and how He tells men of their work and their transgressions and that they have acted defiantly. He also opens their ear to instruction and commands that they change their ways and that if they obey and serve Him, they shall spend their days in prosperity and their years in pleasures. But if they don't, they will die without knowledge.

So, Elihu is explaining that obedience to God gives us knowledge and prosperity, but disobedience will bring destruction and death. In order to obey, we must hear from God. He never promises to perform or bless our works, but His only. We must seek and acknowledge Him in all our ways just as the scriptures teach us. And we must talk to others about the goodness of God, including our children. Elihu proclaimed God's goodness, not his own. He spoke to Job about the majesty of God. He told Job to stand still and consider the wondrous works of God. He asked Job if knew all these things.

Then God began to reveal His omnipotence to Job and told him "to prepare himself as a man. I will question you and you shall answer Me." Then the Lord questioned him about all creation, the earth, the sky, the seas, etc. He humbles Job with His majesty, with questions like "Where were you when I established the foundations of the earth? Who can number the clouds by wisdom? Or who can pour out the bottles of heaven when the dust hardens in clumps, and clods cling together? Who provides food for the raven when their young cry out to God? Have you commanded the morning or the dawn? How about the Leviathan, can you draw him out with a hook? Can you fill his skin with harpoons, or his head with fishing spears? His rows of scales are his pride, shut up tightly as with a seal; one is so near to the other that no air can come between them; they are joined one to another, they stick together and cannot be parted." These and many other examples He spoke to Job for four more chapters.

Then Job answered the Lord and said, "I know that You can do everything, and that no purpose of Yours can be withheld from You. You asked, Who is this, who hides counsel without knowledge? Therefore, I have uttered what I did not understand, things too wonderful for me, which I did not know. Listen, please, and let me speak. You said I will question you and you shall answer Me. I have heard of You by the hearing of the ear, but now my eye sees You, therefore I abhor myself and repent in dust and ashes."

Essentially, Job was saying, as I did that day in the yard, "Oh, I see now, You are God, not me. You, Sir, are Lord of my life, not just on my Sundays and Wednesdays. Not only in the good times, but always. I'm not maintaining my life of righteousness, You are. I'm sorry for trying to live without seeking you and Your righteousness." This is what I refer to as a "Job moment." It is in these times in our lives that we are reminded of just how great our God is and how utterly small we are.

We all have had these times in our lives. Think about them, all the times in your life, whether good or tough, when God has delivered you and taught you something about His goodness in the process. Then remember to tell others, particularly your children about His goodness and how great our God is. Remember Proverbs 20:6, "most men will proclaim each his own goodness, but who can find a faithful man?" There is no greater source of protection than that of our Heavenly Father.

Chapter Five

A Father's Instructions

I nstructions are good. Typically, we receive them from one
who is familiar with a particular subject or a product of
interest. You may, like me, be tempted to do things based on
your own understanding, trying to figure them out as you go,
putting things together without reading the instructions. Since
that is usually the way I did things on my own, why would I be
surprised that my children, and now my grandchildren, do the
same, seldom following instructions provided for them? It
always seemed to me that instructions only slowed me down.

Notice I said, "it seemed to me." Of course, that is not always
true. Following instructions might take a little more time up
front, but in the long run, it can save you from many mistakes.
Have you ever started putting something together for your
children or your wife, just glancing at the instructions and then
jumping right into it as if you knew what to do? If so, you've
probably experienced the frustration of having to start over, or
maybe even messing something up so badly that you can't fix it.
At that point you realize that if you had only taken a few minutes
to read through the instructions, you would already be finished
and ready to move on! Now you are having to start over.

Likewise, can you remember a time of not following the
instructions of your father, and getting yourself into a jam? Did
you wish you would have listened and heeded your father's
instructions? This reminds me of another Bible verse, Proverbs

4:1, "Hear my children, the instruction of a father, and give attention to know understanding." This speaks loudly to me as I reflect on my own life and the many times, I failed to do what he said. Of course, I heard my father's instruction, but notice the verse says to pay attention to what it means. When I do that, I gain a better understanding of the purpose of the instruction. If I'm reading instructions for putting a new toy together for my grandchildren, it usually says to read the instructions all the way through first, and then start to assemble it. How often have we either not read all the way through them, or even read them at all, and then jumped in with both feet as if we knew what to do!

Recently, my wife brought home a new toy for our grandson. She immediately started putting it together - and you guessed it - without reading the instructions. Later, I had to take the toy apart, get the instructions out, read them, and then put it together correctly. Amazing how well it worked once it was put together according to the directions!

As a father, I've given many instructions to my children, and now to my grandchildren. They're not much different than I was as a child. They listen, or at least appear to listen, but seldom follow my instructions. At best, they are bent on finding a shortcut, trying to do it their own way. I now know what if feels like as a parent to give instructions to my children, and then watch them ignore them, just as I did most of my life. As a father, it's painful to watch our children make choices opposite of, or other than, the instructions we have given them. We know the path they are on because all too often we too, have made many of the same decisions, choosing to ignore sound instruction from a father who knows and has experienced life's challenges.

I remember my father many times telling me what not to do, as well as often telling me what to do. I can also remember many times doing what I was instructed not to do, and other times not doing what I was told to do. Both are called disobedience, the opposite of obedience. I was disobedient often enough to learn that disobedience always costs me something, perhaps not immediately, but it always costs. Ephesians 5:6 says, "Let no one deceive you with empty words, for because of these things the wrath of God comes upon the sons of disobedience." The next verse says, "Therefore do not be partakers with them." This letter was written to a group of believers who needed to be reminded of their wealth in Christ. Even though they were believers, they were living like beggars. Paul had to remind them to follow the instructions they had been given and to follow the example they'd been given. In Ephesians 5:1, Paul told them to "Be imitators of God (your Father) as dear children." He reminded them that children look and act like their father. In verse 2, He told them to walk in love, like Christ did, giving Himself for us as a sacrifice to God. His life was a sacrifice to His father God by giving Himself as a sacrifice for us. In verses 3 and 4, Paul instructs, "But fornication and all uncleanness or covetousness, let it not even be named among you, as is fitting for saints; neither filthiness, nor foolish talking, nor coarse jesting, which are not fitting, but rather giving of thanks." (In other words, we should be thanking God instead.) Verse 5, "For this you know, that no fornicator, unclean person, nor covetous man, who is an idolater, has any inheritance in the kingdom of Christ and God."

So, Paul is telling us not to be fooled by empty words which cause the Father's anger to come on the sons of disobedience. Don't run with the crowd who trust in the traditions of men, the voice of our culture, rather than the instructions of our Father God. We used to do that but now we are light in the Lord, so we should live like it. The fruit of the Spirit is in all goodness, righteousness, and truth. Righteousness is simply being in right relationship with the Father. In order to maintain that right relationship, we need to do what is right according to Him and we do that by following His instructions.

The Bible is full of stories of the Father's instructions for His people. After Moses led the people, and later passed, God put Joshua in charge. God had promised Moses and His people a lot of good land, so Joshua now began to take the land that God told them to take. The account of Joshua's conquests is found in Joshua 11:16-19.

"Thus Joshua took all this land: the mountain country, all the South, all the land of Goshen, the lowland, and the Jordan plain, the mountains of Israel and its lowlands, from Mount Halak and the ascent to Seir, even as far as Baal Gad in the Valley of Lebanon below Mount Hermon. He captured all their kings and struck them down and killed them. Joshua made war a long time with all those kings. There was not a city that made peace with the children of Israel, except the Hivites, the inhabitants of Gibeon. All the others they took in battle."

Life is full of many battles. There are God's people and the enemy, and his people, who ignore the things of God and follow their own ways, who worship what they want to when they want to. The Father knew this was not good for His children, so He helped clear the way for His people. Joshua sought the instructions of the Father and did what He heard from the Father. After many years of battles and war, the promise of the Father was fulfilled. Joshua 21:43-45 says, "So the Lord gave to Israel all the land of which He had sworn to give to their fathers, and they took possession of it and dwelt in it. The Lord gave them rest all around, according to all that he had sworn to their fathers. And not a man of all their enemies stood against them; the Lord delivered all their enemies into their hand. Not a word failed of any good thing which the Lord had spoken to the house of Israel. All came to pass."

This is incredible - not one instruction that the Father had spoken had failed! Notice it says that whatever the Lord speaks is good! It may not have seemed good (to us) for them to take over this land, to take it from these people, but it was.

The point is this: The Father knows what is good for His children, and His instructions will not fail.

The bottom line in all this is that it is good to read the instructions, but if you don't do what they say, life doesn't work like it is designed to work. Our Heavenly Father, the Living God, has given us His word in written form of the Holy Bible, and also in the form of a man, Christ Jesus, who was God in flesh. We have both written instructions for life and also an example in human form for us to follow. But He did not stop there. He has even sent as a Helper the Holy Spirit of God to help us, guide us, lead us, and to empower us to walk in His righteousness, and also His love, which has been shed abroad in our hearts.

So now, we have no excuse! It is up to us. Once we have been born again, we are equipped for every good work He has for us. We have all the instruction, power, and direction we will ever need. Now, here comes the *but,* it is up to us to read the instruction manual for life, all of it, and read it continually. It is also up to us to follow the human example we have in Jesus, revealed to us both in the written word, and also by the Holy Spirit revealing Him and His divine nature to us. And it is also up to us to hear instructions from God the Father by the Holy Spirit, instructions which truly are good for us.

You will never really know God the Father or understand the fullness of His love without spending time in His written word, nor know and understand His instructions for the life He has designed for you. Nor will you understand the divine nature of God the Father, revealed in scriptures and the person of Jesus Christ. You will not know His mercy or His truth unless you choose, by an act of your will, to seek Him by reading and hearing His word (the instruction manual for life) and meditating on it in order to hear from the Father, God Himself, who confirms His word to you personally by His Holy Spirit.

You might be thinking, "but I just don't hear from God like some seem to hear." As parents, do we not spend more time talking to the children who actually listen? A father will never stop talking to his children, but he is likely to talk less if he knows his child is not listening.

Two days ago, I got up and prayed first thing, as I normally do, but I specifically asked the Father to establish my thoughts and direct my steps. Here are some things that happened that day after asking my Father for His instructions for the day.

My day started as it typically did. I did some paperwork and worked on plans for a bit. I made and returned some calls, then began making appointments with customers. I finished about 6 pm and left to make a hospital visit downtown. On the way, I passed a homeless woman walking near an intersection. It was extremely hot that day and the humidity was high. I prayed for her as I went through the intersection.

Then I had a phone call from one of my daughters who was having some struggles in a relationship with a man she'd been seeing. She described what they were going through, both her feelings and those he had expressed to her. I listened carefully for several minutes, and then gave her some instructions on what I thought she should do. I explained what I thought her boyfriend was thinking and feeling. She had just told him the relationship was over. She believed other things were more important to him than she was, and she felt he didn't really love her. After I explained to her what I perceived he might be thinking and experiencing, it made sense to her. As I walked into the hospital, I told her I loved her, and we ended the conversation.

After my hospital visit, I left the parking garage, and started toward home, taking the same path I had taken to the hospital.

Once again, I saw the same homeless woman, this time on the other side of the street a few blocks away from where I had seen her earlier. Now she was sitting under a shade tree. I knew how terribly hot she must be walking around in that heat all day. I began praying again and talking to God. *"Lord, how can I show her your love? Where could I take her for her for help? It's too late to go to the day center. I'm sure she's been there before and probably knows about it. If I give her money what would she spend it on?"*

By the time I finished praying, I was on the expressway a few miles away. That's how long it took me to quit talking and start listening. I heard, "cheese puffs." I thought, *Ok, I can do that.* I took the next exit and turned back in her direction, stopping at a store on the way. *What else, Lord, I know she's hot and thirsty?* I heard, "Gatorade." *Ok. Lord, it needs to be good, it needs to be what she likes in order for her to know that this is You and not me.* I said, *How about a name?* I heard, "Loraine," nothing else.

I went into the store, expecting the Lord to direct me to the right stuff. I bought the cheese puffs, some green Gatorade, a deli sandwich, and some fruit. Then I headed back down the street to where I had seen her, hoping she was still there. She was. I pulled into a parking lot near the tree where she was sitting. I grabbed the sack of groceries and put in a small booklet about how to know God. I got out, and as I handed her the sack, I asked her what her name was. She replied, "Elisabeth." I said, "Oh, God had me get these things for you." She said, "God bless you."

I left thinking I must have missed it on the name. The next morning after my quiet time with the Lord, I got dressed, still talking to the Lord. I was thinking about Elisabeth and the Lord said Loraine wasn't her name, but someone she was thinking about, the kind of thing only God could know. I thought, *Wow!*

God, You are so awesome, so amazing, the details You think of! Then I began laughing at how foolish I was not to realize it. Duh! God knows the very thoughts and intents of our hearts. (Matthew 9:4, Hebrews 4:12) I began to think, *Wow! I wonder if Loraine is her mother, or a sister, or maybe a close friend she was thinking of at that very moment. If only I hadn't blown it, she would really know it was God reaching out to her and speaking to her.* I shared this with a close friend, she said God is a God of "overs," so hopefully, I'll get "overs" someday with Elisabeth; but if not me, the Father will send another.

The next morning, my daughter called again. She and her boyfriend had exchanged some emails, and she let me know that my instructions were right on the money. Her boyfriend told her he had been trying to say that very thing to her. He told her, *"I don't know how your dad could have known what I was thinking and feeling, but he did."* Both of these are examples of our Father's instructions. I hope you can see the importance of receiving and obeying His instructions in our lives, and the lives of others.

Chapter Six

Fathers Correct Their Children (Because They Love Them)

"For whom the Lord loves, He corrects,just as a father the son in whom he delights." Proverbs 3:12

I f a father sees his child doing, or about to do, something he knows will harm the child, he corrects him because he loves him and does not want any harm to come to the child. If your toddler is playing in a park, standing on a big rock, and you see him getting too close to the edge, you would quickly correct him or move him back toward the center of the rock to safety. Your toddler probably doesn't understand that you just kept him from harm, nor that you did it because you love him.

Later, there may come a time when that same child gets too close to the edge again, and you don't get there quickly enough. He may fall and get hurt. He may begin to connect the dots. *Hmm, when I get too close to the edge, I fall, and get hurt. I remember when I did that before, my daddy caught me and told me not to get too close to the edge. I remember he said if I fell, I would get hurt. My daddy was right!*

You may be one of those who just did as your father told you to do, and never fell. If so, you are a rare person. Most of us have a rebellious streak in us. We seem to be bent toward doing what we have been told not to do, or we insist on finding out for ourselves. We often prefer to learn by experience rather than by instruction and correction. Why do we have this human tendency? The truth is we inherited it from a man called Adam, whom the Bible tells us was the first man. The Bible also tells us that Adam blew it. He chose, by his own free will, to do what his Father God had instructed him not to do. This is exactly where our rebellious nature comes from.

So, what happens when a child rebels against his father's instructions? He usually gets hurt. Like my dad used to say, *"If you mess with the bull, you will get the horn."* Our actions have consequences. If you willingly choose to do something you've been instructed not to do, you've been warned there will be a price to pay, and it's often painful. Whatever form of discipline your father used - a belt as my dad did, or a paddle, a switch, maybe taking away privileges, or a time out as my daughter does with my grandchildren - whatever form the discipline takes, it costs something, and hurts for a time. The goal of discipline is to bring training, to teach lessons to the child, because the parent loves the child, and wants to prevent future harm. Yes, it's painful to the child in the process, but does not change the fact that you love them. Truly, if you really love your children, you will correct them, just as the verse says.

As a child gets older, the more confident in himself, the more likely he is to assume he doesn't need instruction or correction from anyone else. As a loving father, we must continue to offer instruction. We shouldn't give up because he or she seems to have quit listening. As long as our children are under our care, receiving provision from us, we must also correct them.

There are two parts to this process of correction. One is the giving of the instruction, and the other is the consequences or punishment for failure to follow the instruction. Hebrews 12:5,6 gives an account of Paul's exhortation to Jews who had converted to Christianity and were experiencing persecution (scourging). He reminded them that there is more to be gained in Christ than anything they previously experienced in Judaism. He tells them the suffering they are now experiencing is worth it. In essence, he is saying that if they learn from this, their life will be better than before. Most of us know that if we don't learn by the consequences when we ignore correction, we'll continue to receive those same consequences of our choices.

The truth is that a father's ways are nearly always better than our own. Why? It's because they have experienced more of life than we have. Fathers don't typically offer correction without a reason. They've learned lessons - often painful - by suffering the consequences of not following the instructions they now want us to follow. Their disobedience cost them something that they want to help us avoid.

The trouble with most of us is that we don't believe we need correcting. It's so easy to look around and find someone to compare ourselves with, someone who may make our behavior seem like we're doing pretty well. That makes us feel like we don't really need correction. It happens about the time when we get our lives pretty well cleaned up and we begin to feel too confident in ourselves. After all, we're older, and smarter now. We've experienced life and we are just plain wiser. We start to think, *I've got this figured out now!* And when this happens, it's about time we may need some more correction in our lives.

Do you believe that when your children get out of line you must correct them to get them back in line? Maybe you don't have children, but you can probably remember being corrected yourself. It usually does not feel good. In fact, it can be downright embarrassing and humiliating. It's painful. We seldom like it. After all, why would you like something that hurts? Could it be that the pain is worth the end result?

An athlete or bodybuilder will suffer pain - in fact, self-inflicted pain - in order to achieve a goal, right? He does it because he knows that the end result is good. Achieving his goal of becoming better or stronger costs him pain. Does he like the pain? No, but because he knows what it will produce, he will endure it. Likewise, in business, we sometimes have to sacrifice something for a period of time to achieve the benefits later. It's the principle of investment: spend the time, effort or resource now to receive a benefit later. Spend some to make some - it costs something now.

In a similar way, we have a Father in heaven Who corrects us because He loves us - not because He likes to hurt us but because He knows it will produce something good for us. Paul's writing to the Hebrews went on to say, "And you have forgotten the exhortation which speaks to you as to sons: My son, do not despise the chastening of the Lord, nor be discouraged when you are rebuked by Him; for whom the Lord loves He chastens, and scourges every son whom He receives."

The word *chasten* comes from *chaste (hagnos),* a Greek word which means pure from every fault, or immaculate. It's a condition or state of purity, without fault. The noun in the passage "the chastening of the Lord" is the Greek word *paideia* which means the training of a child, including instruction - hence discipline, correction. We don't like these words. I certainly didn't when I was growing up. But I have learned that the chastening from the Lord is always good for me, so I've learned to endure it. I may not love it, but I love what it produces, much like the bodybuilder or the investor in my examples earlier.

When used as a verb, the Greek word *paideia* becomes *paideuo,* which means to train children, much like our word *education* and usually refers to correction in words, reproving and admonishing. The Lord corrects us by His word, which reproves and admonishes us. The end of that Hebrews passage says, "And scourges every son whom He receives." *Phragelloo* is the Greek word for scourge in scripture that describes what the Romans did to Jesus when they beat Him with a whip and tore His flesh. Scourge is used in this verse as a way of showing us there is a cost in this process of correction. It will hurt, it will not feel good, but it will produce a state or condition of purifying, a cleansing that is absolutely good for us and motivated by the love of the Father.

Of course, there are conditions to this verse, an *if* and a *but*. In Hebrews 12:7,8, Paul writes, "*If* you endure chastening, God deals with you as a son; for what son is there whom a father does not chasten? *But* if you are without chastening, of which all have become partakers, then you are illegitimate and not sons." So, the choice is up to us to endure this correction.

What does it mean to *endure* it? Am I just to put up with it? Am I just to hear it? Hearing correction is not enough, is it? If your child hears your words of instruction but does nothing with it, it doesn't produce what you intended it to do, does it? No, it's only when the child hears it and learns from it, either by doing something differently, or not doing whatever prompted the instruction - then and only then will the correction have produced what it intended. The child must not only hear the correction, but he must receive and do something with it. A wise old saying we've all heard is commonly referred to as the definition of insanity: *If you keep doing what you have been doing and expect a different result, you are probably insane. Put another way, we will always be who we've always been if we always do what we've always done.*

So, why do we tend to not receive correction? I believe it's simple. It's not because we are insane or stupid. It's because we don't understand a Father's love and how to receive it. Until we do, we will continue to be reluctant to receive His correction.

It's really not complicated. All we must do is receive it by faith, the same way we receive everything from the Father. Like our salvation, our healing, answers to our prayers - anything and everything that we receive from Father God is by faith. I mean by this we don't see the results correction produces until we accept it by faith. When we do, we will act on the correction we've received, and it will produce the intended results. If we have not received the correction, we won't believe it, and if we don't believe it, we won't make the changes we've been instructed to make.

In Isaiah 55, the Lord speaks to His children through the prophet Isaiah and pleads with His children to accept the invitation to a life of abundance. He tells them to turn from man's ways and to seek the Lord while He may be found, to call on Him and forsake their way, because His way is better. It is higher and His thoughts are higher than man's thoughts. He gives them examples in the earth for them to relate to, and then God says in Isaiah 55:11, "So shall my word be that goes forth from My mouth: It shall not return to Me void, but it shall accomplish what I please. And it shall prosper in the thing for which I sent it."

I've learned that His word will in fact do just as He says. You can take it to the bank, so to speak. You can rely on it as truth in every circumstance and every situation you face. However, it is up to you and me to hear it and receive it by faith as correction, believing that it will produce something good, and is something that is motivated by love for us. When we receive it by faith, it will prosper in the thing the Lord has sent it for and it will produce a life of abundance for you. So then, don't despise the correction, but receive it, knowing that it is given to you out of love - the Father's love.

Chapter Seven

Fathers Give

F athers give, and give, and give, and give, and give, and give and give. A recent television and radio ad for a diamond described it as "a gift that keeps on giving." That's the type of givers fathers are supposed to be.

I know I personally have fallen short in this area of giving most of my life. When you become a father, you begin to give to your children. You give attention to their care, changing diapers, feeding them, clothing them, but the giving doesn't stop there. It just keeps on going, kind of like another ad, the battery operated bunny who never stops but just keeps on going. Your children keep growing, and so do their needs. They need new clothes, teaching and training about what to do, and what not to do, and then why to do certain things, and why not to do others. They need toys to amuse them and help them learn motor skills. As they grow, they need more coaching and teaching at every stage of development. Their toys get bigger and more expensive: bicycles, toys with power, electronics. They need a car, or motorcycle, and of course, then they need fuel, insurance, batteries, etc. You get the picture. Then comes the wedding, the homes, and then the payback finally comes: grandchildren!

Now you're probably thinking, *"Yeah, now they get to begin this giving thing."* That's true, but I'm also thinking of another form of payback. I'm thinking of what blessings grandchildren are. Somehow things seem to be different with them than with our children. We're not so worried and distracted by trying to make a living in this world and to provide the money it takes for all of life's necessities. Hopefully, at this point, the pace is slower, and there's more time to enjoy the little ones.

However, and to my point of this chapter, you are not done giving just because your children now have the responsibility of giving to their children. Now you get to give some of your time to babysitting your grandchildren ... as well as clothes, toys, etc. You have the picture - you just keep on giving and keep on going.

Giving is not just something we do because we are supposed to - no, it is our nature, passed on to us from our fathers. They gave, and we give. If your father just verbally told you to give, and he hadn't demonstrated it to you, you probably wouldn't be giving. My grandchildren don't understand this giving thing yet; they are more into the getting than the giving. When we are young, we get something given to us, and we understand first, "this is mine." We begin to understand possession. We continue down that path, enjoying receiving and possession, but not paying much attention to the giving, probably because possessing is about me.

But is it more about me, or the one who is giving it to me? This, of course, depends on your perspective. Or could it be it is just good for both of us? From my experience, it feels good to receive something from someone, but it also makes me appreciate the person who was thoughtful enough to give it to me.

Recently, my granddaughter got upset with me when I corrected her about something. When she was about to leave and go home with her mom, she was showing her feelings toward me by refusing to say goodbye or give me our traditional hug and kiss. So, Grammy chimed in and said, "Hey, I know you are mad at your Grandpa, but you're not mad at Grammy, so come here and give me a hug." She did, but still refused me, so I said to her, "OK, I'll just find me another bestest granddaughter to love and to play with and give your playhouse and bicycle to her." She immediately responded; "No that's me!" She had taken possession of that title I had given her, "bestest granddaughter." That title was hers. My wife later remarked how amazed she was that I was able to turn her around as fast as I did. Of course then, we had our traditional group hug before she left, and she decided she still loved me. My point is that as children, we love to receive for ourselves; it is special to us and makes us feel special. Even as we grow older, we still like to receive gifts from others, and they still make us feel special, no matter how old we are.

The Bible teaches something on this matter of giving that seems opposite in a way. It teaches it is more blessed to give than to receive. It also teaches a principle of reaping what you sow as well. These go hand in hand because when you give, you receive blessings and the more blessings you receive, the more you want to give. Luke puts it plainly, Luke 6:38: "give, and it will be given to you good measure, pressed down, shaken together, and running over will be put into your bosom, for with the same measure that you use, it will be measured back to you." Seems pretty simple - give and it will be given to you. But there is more to this than it seems on the surface. I once saw my pastor demonstrate this principle, using a box of cereal. He shook it to settle the box and then pressed it down and then kept adding to it, much like I do when bagging leaves. I keep adding and adding and pressing down until it is full and running over. Notice the verse says it will be put into your bosom (your heart is in your bosom), not in your bank. While it might be put into your bank, if you are giving money (remember Galatians 6:7 says you reap what you sow), but something more is going on here. This is a heart thing - the verse says it will be put into your bosom. I believe this process begins to change our hearts about giving. As we begin to give, something is put into our hearts that grows and grows.

Farmers understand that if they plant corn, from one seed a plant will grow that will produce much more seed. The same thing happens as we give (or plant; we get more of the giving seed put into our hearts, which in this case is the ground or soil. That seed just grows and produces more giving seed in our heart and eventually we like giving more than receiving. On the surface, the statement, "It is better to give than to receive," doesn't seem to make sense, but it only seems that way until we begin to experience this principle - then and only then, will this process become real to us. It is a fact.

This seed must first be received into a fertile soil (heart) before it produces its crop of fruit, which is full of seed. I began this chapter by explaining the concept of a father's love that gives and gives and keeps on giving. Jesus had an encounter at a well with a Samaritan woman, a woman of a different culture. She was going to the well to fill her pots with water, and Jesus asked her for a drink. She was shocked that he even spoke to her. She responded, "Jews have nothing to do with Samaritans." But His response was even more shocking. He told her that if she knew who it was who had asked her for a drink, she would ask Him for living water, and she would no longer thirst. She must have thought, *Wow! I' ll never have to walk down here again to fill these pots!* But of course, this was not what Jesus meant. He was talking about something we call grace.

On the surface, grace seems pretty simple: we define it as getting something you don't deserve or haven't earned to deserve it. That in itself is amazing, but He goes on to say this grace will never run out. This is a well of living water, a well that once you've drunk from, you will never have to go to another well. This one keeps on giving, on and on and on and on and on and on and on. It keeps on going and never runs out. It won't dry up when you slip up. It will always be there. The well the woman had gone to, was a pretty good one; it had been there for a couple of generations, continually providing for her ancestors and her and her family. But as good as it was, it only provided one need. As important as that one need was, water being necessary to survive in this life, it pales in comparison with what Jesus was talking about giving her. He used the example of water to help her see something about God's love and grace. He was showing her that God's well of this grace never runs out, it will always be there. But it was the giving of it that put it all into action.

Let me explain it another way: God's love is the merchandise to be delivered. Giving is the vehicle or truck by which it is transported from the factory (God) to its destination (His children).

Of course, there is no better example of giving than God the Father Who is love, according to 1 John 4:8. And love gives and gives and gives. He gave us life when He made us. He gave us the earth and dominion over it (see Genesis 1 and 2). He gave us the animals and the birds, trees, and plants, water, and all we need to have life on this earth He created. When we hid from Him and refused to listen to Him, He gave us forgiveness and His love through Jesus His Son, given to us to bring us back to God our Father. He also gives eternal life, which is the ultimate well, as He spoke to the woman at the well.

Chapter Eight

Fathers Forgive and Forget

As a father of five and a grandfather of two, I know what it is to forgive and forget in the natural sense of a father-child relationship. There is nothing one of my girls or one of my grandchildren could ever do that would change the fact that I love them. There are many things they do and have done that I am not happy about, but it has nothing to do with the fact that I love them. I would love to have a perfect family, everyone doing what's right, saying what's right, everyone happy and content, not lacking in any good thing. Wouldn't that be awesome? Would that make me love them more? No, it would just make their lives better.

As a young boy in school, like many boys, I had a few fights with other boys, but I think I can honestly say that nearly every one of those later developed into a friendship. Almost every instance I can remember, after the fight was over, we got over our differences and became friends. I can't even remember what started most of the fights. So, I wonder, why did we have to fight in the first place?

The truth is, we didn't. We just chose to settle it that way. I'm certain we could have just forgiven whatever had happened without fighting. Many others did, but we considered that to be "un-cool." Why did others choose not to fight? Maybe they were afraid to fight, at least that's what we assumed. After all, I think all of us were afraid the first time we fought someone. But just maybe they were taught by their parents that you don't repay evil for evil, a principle that the Bible teaches. I know you've heard this one, "Turn the other cheek." *Do what? Let him hit me again?* That's right, that is what it says. I don't know about you, but that doesn't make a lot of sense to me.

However, I have practiced it in a different way and it works. One day, my wife and I were arguing about something. She began making her point boldly, if you know what I mean. She was telling me how it was, so to speak. When it was my turn to give it back, instead of my usual "I can get louder and prove my point response," I looked at her, smiled, and walked out of the room. She says she couldn't believe what happened. She didn't even know what to do with that. It worked - the argument was over just like that!

Forgiveness is something you get that you do not deserve, or something you give to someone when they don't deserve it. The Bible calls this *grace,* often defined as undeserved favor. Do you remember a time as a child when you messed up, and knew you were going to be in big trouble, but instead of punishing you, your parent just talked to you, explained what you did wrong, and then did something cool, like taking you out for ice cream? No? I'll bet if you think hard enough, you can think of at least one example. It normally will have a pretty big impact on someone, because he or she is expecting to get what they deserve - a whipping, spanking, detention, silent treatment, or maybe even worse - but instead, they get something far better - kindness instead of punishment, or retribution. It's powerful!

One way we often deal with differences is to not associate with those who are different. You know, if they act different than you, or eat differently, maybe they sound different, or look different - maybe they worship differently - we avoid them and we don't hang out with them. This is common it's been going on since the beginning of time. We cleverly explain it by the word *culture.*

One of many Bible stories about forgiveness never actually mentions forgiveness, but it implies it. It is a story about two people who meet at a well. One was Jesus, a Jewish carpenter and Son of God; the other, a Samaritan woman. (You may remember this woman from the previous chapter.) Jesus asked the woman for a drink of water. She responded with, "How is it that You, being a Jew, ask a drink from me, a Samaritan woman? For Jews have no dealings with Samaritans." The reason the Jews had no dealings with Samaritans is that many years before, a king had brought foreigners into the city of Samaria among the Jews. These strangers did not worship God in the way the Jews did and did not have the oracles (words of God) to live by. They feared a god, but they made carved images to worship and lived according to their own ways. The Jews despised this, so they had nothing to do with the Samaritans.

You can understand, then, why this woman was surprised that Jesus, a Jew, would even talk with her. She would have been expecting a far different reaction, perhaps an uncomfortable silence with nothing said between them. However, Jesus said, "If you knew the gift of God, and who it is who says to you, 'Give me a drink, you would have asked Him and He would have given you living water.' The woman replied, "Sir, you have nothing to draw with and the well is deep. Where do you get that living water? Are you greater than our father Jacob, who gave us the well, and drank from it himself, as well as his sons and his livestock?" Jesus answered her, "Whoever drinks of this water will thirst again, but whoever drinks of the water that I shall give him will never thirst. But the water that I shall give him will become in him a fountain of water springing up into everlasting life." The woman said to Him, "Sir, give me this water that I may not thirst, nor come here to draw." Jesus told her, "Go and call your husband, and come here." She told Him, "I have no husband," which was true. Jesus said to her, "You have well said, 'I have no husband,' for you have had five husbands, and the one whom you now have is not your husband; in that you spoke truly." She replied, "Sir, I perceive that you are a prophet. Our fathers worshiped on this mountain and you Jews say that Jerusalem is the place where one ought to worship." Jesus said, "Woman, believe Me, the hour is coming when you will neither on this mountain, nor in Jerusalem, worship the Father. You worship what you do not know; we know what we worship, for salvation is of the Jews. But the hour is coming, and now is when the true worshipers will worship the Father in spirit and truth; for the Father is seeking such to worship Him. God is Spirit, and those who worship Him must worship in spirit and truth." The woman said to Him, "I know that Messiah is coming," (who is called Christ). "When He comes, He will tell us all things." Jesus said to her, "I who speak to you am He."

Jesus reached across cultural boundaries and gave the woman something she was not expecting. He engaged in conversation with her, told her things about her that she probably was not too proud of, and then eventually told her that He was the Messiah. Jesus disciples returned and marveled that Jesus talked with a woman! Yet no one said, "What do You seek?" or "Why are You talking with her?"

The woman then left her water pot, went her way into the city and said to the men, "Come see a man who told me all things that I ever did. Could this be the Christ?" Then they left the city and came to Him. The Jews ordinarily would not have given her the time of day, first because she was a woman, and secondly, because she was of a different culture. They automatically considered her a sinner, one they would stay away from. But Jesus overlooked those differences and forgave her and forgot the fact that she was a sinner and offered her the gift of God - living water.

We, today, seem to have some of the same issues that the Jews of those days had. We tend to keep a distance between us and those of a different culture. Many of us so-called religious folks tend to keep our distance from so-called sinners or those who are outside of our churches. This woman at least knew that when the Messiah came, He would tell them all things. She had hope for the future in spite of her past; she believed the Messiah was coming. Sometimes, we have preconceived perceptions of people based on their culture, where they live, what they eat, how they dress, by their tattoos, music, etc. Jesus had a way of looking beyond the outside, ignoring the external, and somehow looking at the heart. He knew this woman had potential, and that deep inside, she was like the Jews. He knew the issue was not what she was doing, or had done, but what she didn't know. If He hadn't spoken to her because of her culture, or the way she looked or dressed, etc., she may never have known the truth. Jesus said to her, "We worship what we know; you people worship what you do not know," and again, "if you knew who I am and who the Father is, you would ask for the living water, and He would give it to you, then you would know." According to Jesus, she wasn't judged for what she had done, but what she knew. He didn't give her what she deserved according to her past, but offered her life - living water that would not run out.

Another story in which Jesus displays forgiveness is found in John, chapter 8. The religious leaders had brought a woman caught in the act of adultery and sat her in the midst of them. They said to Jesus, "Teacher, this woman was caught in adultery, in the very act. We were taught by Moses to stone her, but what do You say?" They were trying to catch Him breaking the laws they were taught so to have something with which to accuse Him. But Jesus stooped down and wrote on the ground with His finger, as though He did not hear. So, when they continued asking Him, He raised Himself up and said to them, "He who is without sin among you let him throw a stone at her first." And again, He stooped down and wrote on the ground. Then one by one, the accusers left, until there was no one left except the woman and Jesus. Jesus said to her, "Woman, where are those accusers of yours? Has no one condemned you? She said, "No one Lord." And Jesus said to her, "Neither do I condemn you; go and sin no more." Then Jesus spoke to them again, saying, "I am the light of the world. He who follows Me shall not walk in darkness but have the light of life."

I have often wondered why it is so easy for me to see other's faults but overlook my own. Have you ever caught yourself complaining about what someone has done, and later realized you had done the same thing, possibly many times? One would think it would be easy for us to overlook other's mistakes when we have done the same things as well or maybe even something much worse. But Jesus had not done anything wrong, had not made mistakes like we all have and yet, He had no problem forgiving others their faults. He just simply said, "Go and sin no more." (In other words, don't do it again. It's bad, so learn from this and don't do it again.) His approach always worked. This is how fathers are supposed to correct their children, forgiving them and correcting them, not by saying "Don't do this or else this is what you are going to get."

I think we have a tendency to think one must change first before we can forgive them or before they deserve our attention or acceptance. I heard a pastor put it this way: "We want to clean the fish before we catch them." That seems a bit backwards, doesn't it? It's obvious you can't clean what you don't have.

I know from broken relationships in my own life experiences, that this is often exactly what we do. We expect one to change first in order to receive our acceptance or forgiveness, but that just does not work. We must first forgive them and eventually they will change.

You may say, "Well, I've done that, but it didn't work." That may be true, but God says that is the right thing to do and He showed us how it does work in these Bible stories. Forgiveness is not an option for God's children, it is a command. It is one of the foundational principles of His love. It is how we come into relationship with Him. We accept His forgiveness and what He did through Jesus dying on the cross for us. Peter, one of the disciples, asked Jesus one time (Matthew 18:21,22) "Lord, how often shall my brother sin against me, and I forgive him? Up to seven times?" (Peter's thinking, *Surely that's enough!*) Jesus said to him, "I do not say to you, up to seven times, but up to seventy times seven." Jesus was saying as many times as it takes, you just keep doing what you are supposed to do, no matter how many times you are mistreated. He was saying *I didn't say to forgive them until they change, I'm saying to forgive them as often as I forgive you and more if that is what it takes.*

He then told them a story which He says is like the kingdom of heaven. A certain king wanted to settle up his accounts with his servants. To one who owed him ten thousand talents, but was not able to pay, the master commanded the servant and his wife and children be sold to settle the debt. The servant then pleaded with his master to have patience with him and he would pay it all. The master was moved with compassion and forgave him the debt. (He wiped it out, took it off of the books.) But then, that same servant, who had just been forgiven the equivalent of $10,000 went out and grabbed one of his servants who owed him an amount equaling $100, took him by the throat, and demanded his money. When his servant asked for patience so he could have time to pay it all, his master would not forgive him and threw him into prison until he could pay the debt. This is an illustration of how we are far too often. But Jesus shows us that Heaven is not like this. Word got back to the Master, the King, and He called the one who was forgiven the $10,000 debt and said to him, "You wicked servant! I forgave you all that debt because you begged me. Should you not also have had compassion on your fellow servant, just as I had pity on you?" And his master was angry and delivered him to the torturers until he should pay all that was due to him. Jesus said, "So My heavenly Father also will do to you if each of you, from is heart, does not forgive his brother his trespasses."

Notice He used the word *torturers.* Have you ever known or experienced yourself how bitter and unhappy someone is when he harbors unforgiveness toward someone else? It is like being tortured. You are miserable, and you will be until you deal with it. You might think this is unfair, but it is completely just, as in the preceding story. God says you can't receive My forgiveness and not forgive others yourself. Remember, God forgives us while He himself is completely free of sin. He has every right to cast stones, but He chooses not to, and He chooses to offer His love to us in His forgiveness.

In Matthew 6, immediately after what we call the Lord's Prayer, Jesus says in verse 14: "For if you forgive men their trespasses, your heavenly Father will also forgive you." Adding in verse 15, "But if you do not forgive men their trespasses, neither will your Father forgive your trespasses." Forgiveness is not an option with God. Furthermore, it is because of His love for us that He requires this of us because He knows that to live in unforgiveness is torture to us. Jesus himself on the day of His crucifixion, after they had nailed Him to the cross, looked up toward heaven and said, "Father, forgive them for they do not know what they do."

Fathers forget. This might seem like a strange statement, but it is true. Actually what we fathers do is we choose to forget certain things just as we choose to remember certain things.

When it comes to our children, we tend to forget any bad thing about our children and remember the good things. For example, don't we tend to remember things like a great play they made on the ball field more than the one they blew? *What one? I remember the one she laid out fully parallel to the ground about four feet above it, stretched as far as she could, caught the ball in the very edge of the pocket of her glove, hit the ground, rolled to her feet, and made the throw for a double play. I remember both teams gave her a standing ovation!*

Remember what one she blew? I can't remember that one.

I remember the time her sister walked out on stage to receive the award of salutatorian of her graduating class. But remember what mistake she made? I don't remember that. I remember the hit her other sister made that started the rally that caused the team to make the State Championship game. I don't remember any strikeouts. I remember my other daughter's first home run. I don't remember any of her strikeouts. I remember when she confided in me, when she needed help and compassion. I don't remember when she ignored my advice and got herself into trouble.

This kind of forgetting just seems to come naturally for a father. The truth is we don't necessarily forget, but we choose not to remember certain things when it comes to our children. God, our Father, in much the same way, says in Jeremiah 31:34, "No more shall every man teach is neighbor and every man his brother, saying 'know the Lord,' for they all shall know Me, from the least of them to the greatest of them says the Lord, For I will forgive their iniquity and their sin I will remember no more." He is speaking through the prophet about His children of the nation of Israel of and Judah, about a new covenant that He will make with them, not like the one He made with their fathers. Under that covenant, their fathers were given a law, the set of rules to live by and to keep, in order to stay in good standing with God. As hard as they tried, they could not keep all the law. So, God came up with a new covenant, not because the law was wrong, but because His children could not keep it.

So, God gave His children grace (forgiveness) and chooses to not remember their sins. He also says they won't have to be taught or encouraged to know Him but because of His grace they will know Him. It will not be because of anything they do, but because of Who He is and what He has done.

Chapter Nine

Fathers Name Their Children

It is customary to give names to our children. As a parent, we spend much time and thought coming up with names for them. I remember not so long ago my daughter's struggle with naming her children. She came up with lots of options, but ultimately, the father made the decision that our first grandchild would be named Baiker, and so, this is our granddaughter's name. I also remember her struggles with naming our grandson, Ryker. She didn't make it final until he was a couple of months old.

Why do we struggle so much with naming our children? I believe it's because we know deep down that names are important. They are a part of our identity, and our name will be what we are known by. I recall naming my girls. Each one took much thought and discussion with my first wife. My first daughter received a portion of my first name as we came up with the name Jonna, similar in the way it's pronounced. We continued with the "J's" as we named our second daughter Jamie. When we were blessed with twins, we had to come up with two names and we chose Jessi and Jerri. I remember thinking, "That's it!" I knew these were to be their names. Then I realized I would have to decide which one would be Jessi, and which one would be Jerri. I was anxious at first, but then I just knew. Jessi was born first, and then came her twin sister, Jerri. Later, came my youngest daughter, Jena. (Again, the "J's" - there's something about the "J" sound for us!)

Later, I gave each of them nicknames. Fathers often like to give their children another name. I went with the "B's" this time, hence Jonna Bonna, Jamie Bamie, Jessi Bessi, Jerri Berri, and Jena Bena. Even as grandfathers, the tradition continues with names like Punkin, Darlin, and my favorites, Bestest Granddaughter and Bestest Grandson.

Of course, each of our daughters have our last name, at least until they marry and receive a new name. Then they will be identified in a new way. Besides being the daughters of the Robertsons, they will be the wives of so and so and receive a new name and identity.

This tradition was started many years ago. When God the Father created man, the first man, He named him Adam. Then he gave Adam all the animals to name, and then a wife, a helpmate to name: Eve. Of course they named their children. The Bible tells us more about this tradition in the many stories throughout the Bible. It reveals that names are given by the Father just as in the beginning with Adam, and then by our natural fathers as with Adam and his sons, and so on. The Bible also shows us that the Father gives us a new name. Let me just tell you in simple words what I've learned from these stories.

Adam had one son, Cain who gave an offering of the fruit of the ground to God, and another son, Abel, who gave of the first born of his flock and its fat to God. The Bible says that God respected Abel and his offering but did not respect Cain and his offering. I believe that from the one who gave from his first and best would have come a line of God's people who continued serving and pleasing God by passing this tradition on. However, Cain, who gave an offering, (but not his first and best) became jealous when God found his brother Abel's gift more pleasing. So, Cain killed his brother Abel. And from Cain then came those who strayed from God and went their own way. Eventually, almost everyone was going their own way and doing what they pleased.

When Adam was one hundred thirty-five years old, he slept with his wife Eve again and she bore a son to him, whom Adam named Seth, "For God has appointed another son for me instead of Abel whom Cain killed." From Seth's line (his seed) came Noah, nine generations later. In those days, men lived much longer and apparently, they only recorded the lineage of the first born. The average age of those nine first borns from Adam to Lamech (Noah's father) was eight hundred forty-seven years. All of these men in the line of Seth had many other sons and daughters, but only the first born of each is recorded. Lamech lived seven hundred seventy-seven years, which is considered to be a perfect number. Men had begun to multiply and had daughters born to them, and they saw their beauty. The Bible actually says in Genesis 6:2 "the sons of God saw the daughters of men that they were beautiful, and they took wives for themselves of all whom they chose." So, God said, "My Spirit shall not strive with man forever, for he is indeed flesh; yet his days shall be one hundred twenty years." I believe maybe God wanted to be the one who chose their wives for them, and not they themselves, choosing all they wanted.

God could not find anyone who served and honored Him and did what He wanted, except for one man, named Noah. So, God took Noah and his family and started over by bringing the flood that wiped out everyone except Noah's family and the animals he took with him on the ark.

After forty days and nights of rain, God caused the rains to cease and brought winds to come on the earth to dry its surface. Then God spoke to Noah and told him to go out of the ark with all the animals and his wife and sons and their wives and to be fruitful and multiply. Noah left the ark and built an altar to the Lord and took of every clean animal and clean bird and offered burnt offerings on the altar. The Lord smelled a soothing aroma and said in His heart, "I will never again curse the ground for man's sake, although the imagination of man's heart is evil from his youth' nor will I again destroy every living thing as I have done." So, God blessed Noah and his sons and told them again to be fruitful and multiply.

Then God again spoke to Noah and his sons (Genesis 9:8-17) and made a covenant with them and with their descendants and every creature on the earth. He told them that He would never again bring floods to destroy all flesh, and that He would put a rainbow in the clouds to be a sign of His covenant to them, and He would remember His covenant with them.

So, from Noah's sons, the earth was filled with many sons and daughters. They each had nations with borders, and they had one language and one speech. As they were traveling from the east, they found a flat piece of ground in the land of Shinar. So, they stopped there and decided to build a city and a tower for themselves. The tower was to reach the heavens, and they said, "Let us make a name for ourselves lest we be scattered abroad over the face of the whole earth." This, of course, was not God's plan; they came up with this plan on their own. They had decided to do what they wanted to do, and not do what God wanted.

God knew that because they all had one language, they would succeed. So, the Lord said, "Come let Us go down and there confuse their language that they may not understand one another's speech." And thus, the Lord scattered them abroad from there over the face of all the earth, and they stopped building the city. God got them back on His plan. He did not want them to settle and build a city together. He wanted them to spread out and multiply and fill the earth. That place became known as Babel, because the Lord confused the language of all the earth and scattered them from there over all the earth. God also did not intend that they make a name for themselves. And He began to unfold more of His plan.

From the line of Shem (one of Noah's sons) came Terah who bore Abram, Nahor, and Haran. Haran died before his father, Terah. Terah took his son Abram and his grandson Lot, the son of Haran, and his daughter-in-law Sarai, Abram's wife, and went out to go to the land of Canaan, but when they came to the land of Haran, they stopped and lived there, instead of going on to the land of Canaan. After Terah died there, the Lord said to Abram (Genesis 12:1-3), "Get out of your country, from your family and from your father's house to a land that I will show you. I will make you a great nation; I will bless you and make your name great and you shall be a blessing, I will bless those who bless you and I will curse him who curses you; and in you all the families of the earth shall be blessed."

Notice what God said. He said, "I will do this," not you. Abram's forefathers took it upon themselves to make a name for themselves instead of doing what God had said. Now, God had chosen to make His covenant with Abram. So, Abram did as the Lord told him. He took his people and went to the land of Canaan. There, the Lord appeared to Abram and said, "To your descendants I will give this land." And, as Noah had done, Abram built an altar to the Lord. Then, he moved to a mountain east of Bethel and west of Aion, pitched his tent and again built an altar to the Lord. Everywhere Abram went, people knew he was a man who followed God. He went where the Lord said to go, and did what the Lord said to do.

When Abram heard that his nephew Lot had been taken captive, he gathered his men, then sought out and defeated those who had taken Lot. He brought back Lot, as well as Lot's possessions, his family, and the people with him. The kings of the area went out to meet Abram after his return from the battle. Melchizedek, king of Salem, was one of them. He was the priest of God. He blessed Abram and said, "Blessed be Abram of God Most High, Possessor of heaven and earth; And blessed be God Most High, Who has delivered your enemies into your hand." Abram then gave a tenth of all the spoils to Melchizedek.

Another king spoke up and asked if he could keep the people and Abram take the goods. But Abram refused and said, "No, I'm not taking anything from you that belongs to you because you might say that it was you that made me rich." Abram knew that it was God who made him rich, because God had promised to bless him and to give him land and possessions. (In other words, God was making a name for him, and Abram knew it.)

After this, the Lord came to Abram in a vision and said, "Do not be afraid, Abram, I am your shield, your exceedingly great reward." (Genesis 15:1) Abram replied, "Lord, what will You give me, I don't have a child and the heir of my household is my servant Eliezer of Damascus!" So, the word of the Lord came to him saying, "This one shall not be your heir, but one who will come from your own body shall be your heir." And He brought Abram outside and said to him: "Look now toward heaven and count the stars if you are able to number them. So shall your descendants be."

And Abram believed in the Lord (he trusted what the Lord had said) and God accounted it to him for righteousness (right standing with God, or right relationship with God). I believe Abram just trusted what God said more than what things looked or seemed like. Then God told him, "I'm the Lord, who brought you from where you were to give you this land to inherit it." He was saying, "this is My plan for you, I'm working it - don't worry, I've got it covered."

However, after many years, Sarai (Abram's wife) got impatient and took the matter into her own hands. She pleaded with Abram to have a child with her maidservant, an Egyptian named Hagar, which he did. When Hagar conceived, Sarai became jealous, even before the child was born and was cruel to Hagar, so much so that Hagar fled. But the Lord sent an angel to Hagar to comfort her and to send her back to Sarai to give her a son. The Lord told her that the son would be named Ishmael. Hagar gave them a son when Abram was eighty-six years old.

When Abram was ninety-nine, the Lord appeared to Abram and said to him, "I am Almighty God, walk before Me and be blameless. And I will make My covenant between Me and you and will multiply you exceedingly." Abram fell on his face and God talked with him, saying, "As for Me, behold, My covenant is with you, and you shall be a father of many nations. "No longer shall your name be called Abram, but your name shall be Abraham; for I have made you a father of many nations. I will make you exceedingly fruitful; and I will make nations of you, and kings shall come from you. And I will establish My covenant between Me and you and your descendants after you in their generations, for an everlasting covenant, to be God to you and your descendants after you. Also, I give to you and your descendants after you the land in which you are a stranger, all the land of Canaan, as an everlasting possession; and I will be their God." (Genesis 17:1-8)

(You might be thinking, *Why wait until Abram is ninety nine?* I believe God was preparing him. He knew that in order for Abram to become the father that He wanted him to be, Abram would need to completely trust in the Lord.)

God the Father was telling Abram his new name, the one He had chosen for him: Abraham, which literally means "a father of a multitude." The name Abram meant "exalted father." Abram got his new name from God the Father. Names are important. God was making a name for Abram, not Abram making a name for himself. When God said, "I have made you a father of many nations," He gave Abram a new name, which was the one in which God would fulfill His plan.

Names are more than just a way of identifying who one is or what he is called. Names can also signify a reputation. For example, have you known a family who seemed to all have the same occupation or skill, perhaps soldiers, doctors, brick masons, carpenters, steel or ironworkers, miners, etc.? By their names, they had more than just name recognition, they also had a reputation by their name. In Abraham's day, his language was Hebrew, and the word for "name" was *Shem,* which could be used for reputation, for fame (which may include power), and for memory (what one is remembered by). It could even describe inheritance, which may include property. It was probably no accident that Abram came from the line of Noah's son, Shem.

This sheds some light on what God the Father was doing with Abraham. He was giving him a name with meaning, an inheritance which included all of the meanings of the word for name, *Shem.* This name would be remembered as the father of many nations (a memory), of fame (you shall be My people, God's family), of inheritance (the land he was given by the Father, and of power (an everlasting possession). In other words, God was saying, *"a name that you, Abraham, will be known by, remembered by, and with this name you get this special piece of land which will be yours and your descendants forever. This is powerful and no one can take it from you because I gave it to you forever. By this name you will be known, not by your former name. So, I have done My part. We have a deal, a contract (covenant). Your part is to keep it - you and your descendants after you, (all your kids and their kids), to keep it going, to pass it on.*

Then God told Abraham, "I'm also going to give your wife Sarai a new name: it shall be Sarah, Hebrew for princess. She'll be a mother of nations and kings of peoples shall come from her." Abraham first fell down laughing, and then said, "Shall a child be born to a man who is one hundred and shall Sarah who is ninety bear a child?" Then he said, "Oh that Ishmael might live before You!" Then God said "No, Sarah, your wife, shall bear you a son, and you shall call his name Isaac: I will establish My covenant with him for an everlasting covenant, and with his descendants after him." (Genesis 17:17-19) God had a plan for this name to be passed on, and it was to be through the son that He had given Abraham and Sarah, not through the son that was from the Egyptian maidservant and Abram (the former man). God was saying, *this is something that I am doing, not you, and you are doing it My way, not yours.*

God said to Abraham, "I have heard you concerning Ishmael, and I have blessed him, and I will make him fruitful and will multiply him exceedingly. He shall beget twelve princes, and I will make him a great nation. But My covenant I will establish with Isaac, whom Sarah shall bear to you at this set time next year." (Genesis 18:17-19) And the Lord said, "Shall I hide from Abraham what I am doing, since Abraham shall surely become a great and mighty nation, and all the nations of the earth shall be blessed in him? For I have known him in order that he may command his children and his household after him, that they keep the way of the Lord, to do righteousness and justice, that the Lord may bring to Abraham what He has spoken to him." Here the Lord has revealed His purpose, choosing to have relationship with him and giving Abraham his new name: It was to pass it on to his children that the Lord had given him. Remember, the Lord had said to him, "I will make you a father of many nations." This would be his legacy, his reputation, a part of what Abraham would be known for, and more importantly, God would be their God, and they would be His people.

So, God the Father began unfolding His plan to make Abraham a father of many nations. From his son Isaac, the one with whom God the Father had said He would establish His covenant, came Jacob and from Jacob came Judah, and so on. After fourteen generations, from Jesse came David, the king. From David, came Solomon and many after him. Fourteen generations later, God's people were taken to Babylon in captivity. Fourteen generations after that, came the Christ.

But there is something very different about this man, the Christ. His father Joseph was from the line of Abraham and David. His mother was Mary. However, the Bible says Joseph and Mary had not known each other, meaning they had not conceived a child in the normal way a man's seed and the woman's egg would unite to conceive a child. God spoke to Mary and Joseph individually and let them know that she was pregnant by the Holy Spirit. An angel of the Lord told Joseph in a dream that he should not be afraid but to take Mary his wife, saying "She will bring forth a Son and you shall call His name Jesus, for He will save His people from their sins." (Matthew 1:20, 21)

This was what the Lord had spoken through His prophet Isaiah hundreds of years earlier, "Behold, the virgin shall be with child, and bear a Son, and they shall call His name Immanuel, which is translated, 'God with us.'" (Isaiah 7:14) Israel, (the family of God), had heard for hundreds of years through God's prophets that the Messiah was coming to them. "Messiah" means "anointed one." It had signified in their past the reception of the Holy Spirit. But even though they had heard of this for many generations, when the blessing came, the Messiah, the Savior of the world, the people did not believe it was Him. He just didn't look like what they had imagined in their minds. They could not believe God would choose a lowly family to bring Israel's King to them. They must have expected royalty, not a child born to a poor family.

Yet it was true, this was the Messiah. Jesus lived a sinless life and went about doing the will of His Heavenly Father, but Israel did not believe in Him, and eventually had him killed on a cross. But this, too, was part of God's plan to give Him a name above all names. "Who being in the form of God, did not consider it robbery to be equal with God, but made Himself of no reputation, taking the form of a bondservant, and coming in the likeness of men. And being found in appearance as a man, He humbled Himself and became obedient to the point of death, even the death of the cross. Therefore God has highly exalted Him and given Him the name which is above every name, that at the name of Jesus every knee should bow, of those in heaven, and of those on earth, and of those under the earth, and that every tongue should confess that Jesus Christ is Lord, to the glory of God the Father." (Philippians 2:6-11)

As Jesus humbled Himself, God exalted Him, raised Him up, and gave Him the name above all names. God is working His plan to save His people from their sin. Previously, when people would sin, God had established a way for them to atone for the sin. He would have them bring a male animal, a sheep or lamb, without blemish (perfect) and give it to the priest, and the priest would burn it on an altar for a sacrifice for the atonement, forgiveness, of their sin. (Leviticus 1)

Now, God was instituting His replacement for this continual need of His people to be forgiven for their sin. He sent His son Jesus to be the sacrifice for the atonement, forgiveness of all of mankind's sin. Paul put it this way, in Romans 5:17, "For if by one man's offense death reigned through the one, much more those who receive the abundance of grace and of the gift of righteousness will reign in life through the One, Jesus Christ." Paul was referring to Adam, the first man to sin, and who introduced sin to the world, and by doing so, brought death. In much the same way, Jesus - one man, God coming as a man - by the death of His body, his flesh, made atonement, provided forgiveness for all man's sin, and by doing so, gave us all a way to be reunited with our Heavenly Father forever.

The name of Jesus is the key to our salvation. His name, Jesus, means "savior" and the scriptures in the Bible tell us that it is in His name that we must believe in order to receive forgiveness of sin and everlasting life. John 1:12 says, "But as many as received Him, to them He gave the right to become children of God, to those who believe in His name." Act 4:12 says, "Nor is there salvation in any other, for there is no other name under heaven given among men by which we must be saved."

The Bible refers to His name much like we do to our names; most of us have three names which make up our full name. Mine, for example, is John Charles Robertson; each of these names means something or identifies something about me. John was my father's name, Charles was his father's name, and Robertson is the name by which all three of us are known, as well as the rest of the members of our family, our wives, kids, etc. In a similar way, Jesus has a full name, typically Jesus Christ the Lord. Jesus, meaning "the Savior," Christ, meaning the "High Priest," the one who presents us to God (Hebrews 4:14), and Lord, the "One in whom all authority has been given." In Matthew 28:18, Jesus said to His disciples, "All authority has been given to Me in heaven and on earth." Authority indicates one in power. There is power in His name.

Much like God the Father's plan with Abram to give him a new name, Abraham, meaning "the father of many nations," God's plan for His people is to give them an inheritance through the name of Jesus Christ our Lord. God the Father has passed on the name of Lord to His son, Jesus, just as He had told Abraham it was His purpose in giving him his new name to pass on to his children. And like His promise many years earlier to Abraham to make him a father of many nations, He has kept His word and done it. And to all who will receive it, He has given us the name of Jesus, the name that is above all names. This name, which gives us the right to become children of God the Father is ours, it is a gift and a promise from The Father, given to all, as many as will receive it. Like any gift, it must be received in order to take possession of it.

You might think you don't deserve this name. You are right. You don't deserve it, any more than I did or any of us do. But the truth is that fathers don't give gifts to their children because they deserve them, they give gifts because of their love for their children. Fathers don't give meaningless gifts to their children, but good gifts that are good for them and that will give them happiness and joy. The scriptures say that every good and perfect gift is from above, and comes down from the Father of lights, with Whom there is no variation or shadow of turning. Of His own will, He brought us forth by the word of truth, that we might be a kind of first fruits of His creatures. (James 1:17,18) This is the Father's will for us in order for us to pass this name to others, especially to our children whom He has blessed us with.

We all go through life, for a season trying to make a name for ourselves, some of us longer than others. Many who seem to have made a name for themselves discover at the end of their lives that what they had made for themselves was meaningless. They did not realize they could have chosen a name from their Heavenly Father that would be a name of significance and is everlasting. Perhaps their fathers didn't have this name to pass it on, but the truth is, they heard about this name at some point, as we all have. It is up to us individually to receive this gift of eternal life that comes with and through the Name of Jesus which is above all names. **Philippians 2:9**

My prayer for you is that if you have not made the decision before, or if you feel you are not right with God, and the Holy Spirit is whispering to you now, that you will listen to Him and do what He is calling you to do. As I explained earlier, it was one day a couple of years ago that I heard the words from Him to write this book. If I hadn't done what I heard, you would not be reading this book today. So, if you are hearing Him now, I encourage you to heed what you are hearing and receive His love now. He's waiting for you, with the gift of His name.

If this is the desire of your heart, here is a prayer for you to whisper to Him:

"Father, I confess that I have tried to make a name for myself. I've gone my own way in life, and I have not been the person You created me to be. I know You love me in spite of my sin, and that You sent Your Son Jesus to pay the penalty for my sin because of Your love for me. You raised Him from the dead to be Lord of my life.

I confess today that Jesus is Lord of my life. I believe it in my heart. Come into my heart today and make me the person You created me to be. I thank You, Father in the name of Jesus, the Name in which You have given me Your inheritance."

Chapter Ten

Fathers Intercede
For Their Children

To intercede is to act on one's behalf, to mediate on behalf of another's will. Romans 8:27 explains: "Now He who searches the hearts knows what the mind of the Spirit is, because He makes intercession for the saints according to the will of God."

Just as we fathers intercede on our children's behalf, our Heavenly Father also intercedes for us. Have you ever interceded for your children when they did not know what to do in a certain situation? Of course you have. If you are not a father or a parent, you probably have done it for a friend or maybe even a friend's child. We all need intercession throughout our lives. As we go through life's experiences and situations, we encounter things that we don't understand and have never experienced, often things that are far too big for us, and we wonder what to do.

When children are learning how to ride a bicycle, they don't know how to get started without instruction, but after they get started, they will come up against other challenges, like how to stop or how to avoid hitting something. I remember interceding by grabbing the handlebars and steering to slow them down. Perhaps you have taught someone to drive an automobile and you had to do something similar? If you're like most of us these days, there are instructors who sometimes even have an extra set of brakes and maybe even another steering wheel to use to intercede for them. Young people often don't know what to do in every situation, and they may wonder what their father would do in a given situation.

Maybe you can relate in a more personal way, such as a time when someone interceded for you. Perhaps you were at your wit's end with one or more of your children, possibly even multiple times. You may have been at a point where you just didn't know what to do. Maybe you felt that you'd tried everything, and said all you knew to say, and it just didn't seem to work.

Or, have you ever wanted to help a friend, or someone else close to you, and you just didn't know where to begin? Maybe you wanted to pray for them, or for a particular situation, but you just didn't know how or what you should pray. This is what Paul was writing about in Romans 8:26, "Likewise, the Spirit also helps in our weaknesses. For we do not know what we should pray for as we ought, but the Spirit Himself makes intercession for us with groanings which cannot be uttered." He's saying that you don't even know how to ask or what to ask. He's saying you should, but you don't. "So, don't! Allow Me," says God, your Heavenly Father.

This is much like your earthly father or parent has done many times in your life, maybe even as an adult. If my parents had not interceded in my life, I'm certain I would not be sitting here writing this chapter of this book this morning. When I was a teenager growing up with my father in a relatively small town, I was not closely supervised. I had a "long chain," meaning I was allowed to make too many decisions on my own. My father was often gone at night, so I would do pretty much what I pleased, according to my own will. At the time, I looked at it as extra freedom, exactly what most teenagers want. Unfortunately, I was not able to make too many wise decisions at that age. I began drinking, staying out late, driving without a license, and eventually experimented with the popular drugs of the time. All of this, of course, brought trouble into my life.

One night, I had been out drinking and running around town, as did my younger brother. He was sixteen and I was seventeen at the time. He was out with one of his best friends and a couple of girls. He had gone to take his friend home, and I knew where he would be afterwards, so I went to an intersection to wait for him and his girlfriend. I pulled to the side of the road at a stop sign, and a few minutes later, they pulled alongside of me. We talked for a minute or so when his friend who had gotten his own car came flying over the hill and smashed into the back of my brother's car. It exploded into flames immediately. His friend was unhurt and quickly got to my brother's car, opened the passenger door, and retrieved my brother's girlfriend. However, my brother was trapped by the steering wheel and could not be freed from the burning car.

I'd never felt so helpless. I didn't know what to do or even how to deal with my feelings. People tried to comfort me, but I rejected it all. I didn't want to talk to anyone. I think I just wanted to forget it. Of course, I felt guilty and responsible. Sometimes I still do. After that, I kept doing stupid things like driving and drinking. I wrecked two cars and totaled them. Fortunately, no one was hurt.

It was shortly after the second one that I graduated from high school, and shortly after that my parents interceded in my life. My mother and stepfather were living in Tulsa, so I was told I would have to live with them for a while. They were living a very different lifestyle than I was used to, and they began trying to help me adapt to their lifestyle. While it did not sit well with me, it probably saved my life. Had they not stepped in and interceded, I'm certain I would not be here today.

The point of this story is to help you relate to the fact that we don't know what we should concerning the things of life. The Bible says that *none* of us do. When I was much younger, I thought everything was about me, myself, and I. So, as I proceeded to live just like that, it got me into much trouble. I hurt many others. Much like I needed intercession back then in my life to keep me from harm and trouble, I still need it to keep me on the right road and to keep me from making wrong turns. God, my Heavenly Father, has used people, including my earthly parents, throughout my life, to intercede on my behalf in order to achieve His will and plan for my life - not my will and plan, but His. Of course, the reason He has had to use others is because for many years, I had no personal relationship with Him. I had no conversation with Him, except maybe for an occasional one-way conversation like "Help me, God!"

What Paul is writing about in Romans 8:26 is for those who have this personal relationship with their Father, with the intercession of the Holy Spirit, revealing the Father's will to us. Paul said we ought to know how to pray, but we don't, so the Holy Spirit intercedes for us. Recently, I experienced this in my life. One morning on my way to work, as I began to reach for my radio button, I heard a voice from inside me saying, "No, let's talk some more this morning." Earlier that morning, I had a time of prayer and devotion in reading the Bible. I was on my way to meet with a group of men, most of who were in the construction business, an industry that had been hit very hard with economic woes at that time. I began to pray in the Spirit for a few minutes, then prayed with my understanding, particularly about those who were affected by the troubles in the construction industry, and specifically for this particular group of men. I then saw myself speaking to a larger group of builders and contractors.

I had been on the road approximately six to eight minutes when I passed through a small town in which there were a very large number of needy people. I began to pray a bit in understanding, saying something like, "God I know You love these people and that You have a plan for them. I know You desire to reach them and to have a personal relationship with them. Help me to do whatever my part is." Then I prayed in the Spirit again for a few minutes. Afterward I saw another vision of myself standing before a gathering of those needy people and delivering a message of hope to them.

This all happened in less than half an hour. Later that morning, I thought maybe I should do something about this. One of the men in the group I was meeting with was a past president of the Homebuilders Association, so at breakfast, I asked him if they ever had anyone give their personal testimony before the Association. He said, "No, not as far as I know." I thought, "That's my part." The next day, I received a call from a man I knew who happened to be on the board of a Community Outreach in that small town I prayed about the day before. He asked me to consider and pray about being a member of that Community Outreach. I said, "Okay, I'll do that." I called him in a day or so and accepted the invitation.

At the next meeting, my nomination was accepted by the rest of the board.

A couple of months later, during a meeting with another group I meet with regularly on Wednesdays, we were planning an event to reach people who do not yet have a personal relationship with God. The leader asked who or what group should we make our target in terms of a guest speaker to invite to speak to a particular industry. It was quiet for a moment, and I spoke up and suggested we try to get someone in the building and construction industry, because of the tough times all those in the industry were struggling with, which affected a huge

John Robertson

number of the population. This particular group had many national ties to very successful leaders, so we decided to look at our contact lists for a well-known builder who would attract the interest of many, who might be interested enough to accept an invitation to a breakfast or lunch to hear his or her story.

A couple of weeks later we met again, and the leader said they had looked at their list of leaders and businessmen and came up with no one on the list. I was shocked. In the past, we had been able to get well-known speakers from almost any industry or business. He went on to say, "But, we do have a suggestion; we think you are the guy." He was looking at me and calling my name. Now, I was really shocked! The thought had not occurred to me because we always had chosen someone well-known and successful. While I've been blessed in business, I certainly didn't fit the mold of the normal speaker. They asked me to prayerfully consider being a keynote speaker at the next event.

I did and accepted the offer later. We began planning the event by setting a date and praying about those we'd invite. I spent hours in preparation for the upcoming event, trying to write an outline for a speech about the industry which would also include some of my personal story, such as who I was before I knew the Lord, and how a personal relationship with Him had changed my life and my perspective in business.

A couple of months passed, and the date arrived. I stood in front of a group of men and women and shared my story. The group was rather small, only about fifty-five guests, but for me to stand and speak to a group of that size was big for me. At the end of the event, I offered prayer for them to receive Jesus as their Lord and Savior, and a few of them did pray to receive the Lord.

The week prior, I was to have attended a board meeting at the Community Outreach, which met every third Thursday of the month. Not realizing it happened to be a month with five Thursday, I missed the meeting. During that meeting, the man who called me to be on the board asked for someone else to give the devotion at the monthly outreach meal for the needy of the community. My stepfather, who was on the board said, "John would like to do that." So, he called me and told me he had volunteered me to give the devotional that month. So that Thursday, I stood in front of those needy people in the small community and delivered a three minute message of hope.

So, here's a summary of what happened: In one morning, in just half an hour, God the Father revealed His will and plans to me, by intercession of the Holy Spirit, concerning these two groups of people. The only thing I understood was the small glimpse He gave me of me standing in front of those groups. I did not know what to pray for or about, or how it would come to pass, nor all the people that would be involved in making it happen. I knew none of the details, but the Holy Spirit did, and through intercession, He brought them to pass. He revealed those visions to me in less than half an hour. Then after four or five months passed, He brought both visions to pass in the same week. I had almost nothing to do with making these visions come to pass. God said that we don't know what we ought to pray, so the Spirit of God makes intercessions for us - again because we don't know how to pray as we should concerning His will.

This subject is so misunderstood by the majority of Christians and non-Christians. It has become abundantly clear to me that this prayer language (praying in the Spirit) is for God to get His will done here on this earth for His people to be used by God for His purposes in order to reach those who will become His children. The key to this is according to Paul's writing in Romans 8:1-11: to not be carnally minded but to be spiritually minded, which means to think more about the things of God than your things, or the things as he explains that are of the flesh. I wanted to listen to the radio that morning (my flesh wanted that), but the Holy Spirit of God spoke to my spirit, and I heard His voice and yielded to it. That is all my part was until I spoke to those groups.

I might add another note for those of you whom He might ask to do something similar. Once I began speaking, the Lord took over for me and spoke through me what He wanted at the meetings, and He reached the people He wanted to reach. I probably did not read two paragraphs from my notes in forty minutes of speaking.

Many of God's people are not experiencing God's best because of their flesh. They think it is just too weird to open their mouth and speak in languages they do not know; they are too concerned about what their flesh, their own inner voice, is telling them how foolish they sound or how foolish they might look if someone were to see their lips moving when they don't appear to be talking to anyone but themselves. After all, that is just not "right" in most people's way of thinking. But the Bible says, "For we walk by faith, not by sight." (2 Corinthians 5:7) It does not matter what it looks like or feels like.

When we speak in an unknown tongue (language), the Bible says we speak to God and not to men. (1 Corinthians 14:2) Paul says it is better to speak to men in something they can understand so they can get something from hearing it in their understanding. So, speaking in an unknown tongue is meant to be a language or a way of communicating with God about His will, not ours. Remember, He said we ought to know how to pray, but we don't, so the Spirit intercedes on our behalf.

When I get up each morning, I don't know what all will happen that day, nor do I know who will cross my path, or what they might be facing, or going through, but God says through Paul in Romans 8:27, "Now He who searches the hearts knows what the mind of the Spirit, is because He makes intercession for the saints according to the will of God." (Not according to the will of man.) Unfortunately, our will does not line up with His yet. So, He must make intercession for us. You know, the truth is that if the Father had given me the details in my own language so that I understood all He wanted done that day, I would have tried to do something according to my own understanding and messed it up. The result would have been too much of me and not enough of Him. I should be more like Him, but the truth is I'm not, therefore I need His intercession.

As I watch my children grow into young adults and even parenthood now, their will seldom lines up with my will for them. They have not experienced life as much as I have. They don't know what is best for them, even though they are convinced they do. In the same way, I don't know what to ask for from the Father God, because I knot know what's best for me, even though I think I do. He knows us much better than we do, and His will for us is far better than our own will in our lives. In Isaiah 55:8,9 the Lord says, "For My thoughts are not your thoughts, nor are your ways My ways. For as the heavens are higher than the earth, so are My ways higher than your ways, and My thoughts than your thoughts."

He's saying His ways are more important and better than yours. I can tell you without a doubt it is true. I've experienced life my way and a little bit of life His way, and that little bit is far better than my previous forty years or so. Back in Romans 1:18, Paul writes about going from suffering to glory. He is talking about suffering the things of the flesh while we are in our earthly bodies, until we receive our glorified bodies in the age to come. However, there is a direct correlation between this and the suffering of our will for the Father's will. (Simply put, this is not doing what we purpose to do, but what He desires us to do, just as I did that day when I heard His voice in my spirit saying, "No, let's talk some more before you turn on the radio.") God is speaking to our spirits constantly, but we are usually so consumed by our own agendas, routines, and schedules, that we seldom hear Him and many times hear but get distracted and wind up not doing what we heard. This is what Paul was describing as being carnally minded rather than spiritually minded. We spend more time things of the things of this world than the things of God.

Maybe you have not received the Holy Spirit in your life. You might be wondering as you read this, how does one receive the Holy Spirit? Luke 11:9-13 explains one of the ways to receive the Holy Spirit and it happens to be the way I received Him in my life. It is not the only way, according to the Bible, but it is one of the ways. Verse 9 says, "So I say to you, ask, and it will be given to you; seek, and you will find; knock, and it will be opened to you." You start the process by asking, then by looking for it and finally by persistence. He explains, in verses 11-13, "If a son asks for bread from any father among you, will he give him a stone? Or if he asks for a fish, will he give him a serpent instead of a fish? Or, if he asks for an egg, will he offer him a scorpion? If you then being evil, know how to give good gifts to your children, how much more will your heavenly Father give the Holy Spirit to those who ask Him!"

One day a few years ago, after hearing some teaching on this, I sat in my office alone. I had been seeking, but I had not asked specifically for the Holy Spirit, so that day, I did. The minister who taught this said ask for Him and receive Him by faith, just as you received your salvation by faith, so I did. He also explained that you must also by faith open your mouth, and begin speaking by faith, so I did. He explained that most folks receive the Holy Spirit and are afraid to operate in their new prayer language, because it sounds strange to them, or they think they are not doing something correctly. **"And they were all filled with the Holy Spirit and began to speak with other tongues, as the Spirit game them utterance." Acts 2:4** Doubt and fear are both opposing forces to faith. Faith cannot operate in fear, it is opposite. And the Bible says: "But without faith, it is impossible to please Him, for he that comes to God must believe that He is, and that He is a rewarder of those who diligently seek Him." (Hebrews 11:6)

This verse points out not only that God has rewards for those who diligently seek Him, but also we must believe He is God, not that He merely exists. If we believe that He is God, our Lord and Supreme Authority, and not just believe that He exists, we will be much more likely to hear, recognize, and yield to His voice and then experience His best for us, His will.

If you have not asked for the gift of the Holy Spirit, I would encourage you do so. Perhaps you have not even received the gift of salvation, or if you have but you feel like you're not close to Him like you once were, you can start over today. Romans 10:9,10 says;

> "If you confess with your mouth the Lord Jesus and believe in your heart (not your head) that God has raised him from the dead, you will be saved. For with the heart one believes unto righteousness, and with the mouth confession is made unto salvation."

My head might lie to me, and tell me I don't believe, or question my belief, but the scripture says I don't have to believe what my head says but say with my mouth and believe in my heart. Verse 8 of Romans 10 refers to it as "the word of faith which we preach." This is the confession or what you say to receive Jesus as the Lord of your life. It starts this life of faith and it saves you from yourself and the devil himself and all of the schemes he has used to keep you from the life God has planned for you. John 10:10 Jesus explains, "The thief does not come except to steal, to kill and to destroy. I have come that they may have life, and that they may have it more abundantly."

If the devil has been stealing from you, trying to kill and destroy you, you can stop his ability to have authority in your life by accepting what Jesus has done for you and for all those who will receive. The Bible says this salvation is a gift that you cannot earn, the righteousness that we are to believe unto is right standing in the sight of God and Jesus is the only One worthy of that. The Bible says He is the only way. (John 14:6) The Bible also teaches that man is sinful and therefore separated from God and goes on to say that not some of us, but all have sinned and fallen short of the glory of God. (Romans 6:23, and 3:23) This is why God has made a way for us to return to Him through accepting what Jesus has done for us. "But God demonstrates His own love toward us in that while we were still sinners, Christ died for us. (Romans 5:8) It is not enough to just believe that God exists or even to believe all these verses - you must still receive it by faith and confession.

Not too many years ago, I prayed a prayer like this that changed my life from a life of destruction to a life of abundance, from my ways to His ways. If this is your desire today, just pray this prayer:

Lord Jesus, I confess that I have not lived the life You came to give me. I know that this is sin. I believe You do have a wonderful plan for my life, and that for this reason, God the Father sent You to die for my sins. I believe that You were buried and on the third day God the Father raised you from the dead to be my Lord. I ask You today to come into my heart and make me the person You created me to be. Be Lord of my life and help me to experience the life You came to give me.

Thank You, Father,
In the name of Jesus, Amen.

Just as our fathers intercede in our lives, so does our Heavenly Father. If you prayed this prayer today, know that Your Heavenly Father heard you and has interceded in your life to call you into a personal relationship with Him. It is extremely important that you get started correctly in this relationship. You should tell someone whom you believe to be a Christian brother or sister. You should get plugged into a group of like believers. Now that you have a personal relationship with your Creator, you can pray to Him for guidance in where you should attend church.

You should begin every day by thanking God in your prayers and then spending some time reading His word in the Holy Bible. This is how your relationship is maintained and grows into what He intends it to be. When you sit down to read, find a quiet place without distractions and ask God to reveal Himself to you as you read His word. Hide His word in your heart so you will have it when you need it, whether for you or for someone else. If you prayed that prayer, let me say, "Welcome to the family of God, His kingdom, and rule in your life." I promise you it is far better than the life you've known thus far. As one of my brothers likes to say, "Better, better, better!"

Chapter Eleven

The Power of a Father's Love

Power, generally speaking, means strength; it can also mean ability to do something or enabling to do. A simple example of power is illustrated by electricity, such as with the operation of a fan. When an electric fan is plugged in to a source of electricity, it has power to operate and does. If you were to unplug it from its source, it would slow and eventually stop for lack of power. We can easily witness the power of electricity by simply flipping a light switch on and presto, there is light. Flip it off and it's dark. You might prefer the illustration of a gasoline-powered engine or a jet engine; there is something about the sound of that power that you just know, "man, that sounds powerful," and it is. Or, like when fortythree race cars rumble around the track in their pace laps before the race, each one having eight hundred horsepower under the hood - that's an illustration of power! Or, maybe you like aviation and for you, the sound like a jet taking off is the sound of power- wow!

Whatever you think of when it comes to power, it pales in comparison to the power of a father's love. It is truly a source of power. I shared a story in an earlier chapter about a young teenage girl who was out with some friends one evening. Her friends wanted her to join them in doing something that she knew her daddy would not approve of, so she refused. When she refused to take part in their activity, she immediately was attacked with accusations from her friends, like, "You're just afraid you will get caught." She replied, "No, I just don't want to hurt my daddy." What an illustration of the power of a father's love!

I know you're probably thinking that it sounded more like an illustration of the daughter's love than the father's. No, let me explain. While it is about the daughter's love for her father, it is more about a father's love, who first loved her. It was his love for her that prompted a response of love from her. Her father had obviously loved her so much that she knew it, and therefore her response was what she had received from her father. The Bible says you shall reap what you sow. As we give love, we receive it. We don't receive love by demanding it simply because of our authority as a father.

The power of our Heavenly Father's love is far greater than any other display or example of power, even more powerful than His voice and His words - even words that can shake the earth and have power to create all there is. Yes, it was His word that created, and it was His word sent to us that saves us. But it was all motivated by His love. His divine plan of salvation for His people, His creation of the beauty of all we see in the details of His creation, His desire to relate to His children made in His own likeness, and even His wrath and correction are motivated by His love. It is His divine nature of love that makes Him the source of all power. Without Him, nothing was made and without Him nothing will live.

As I write these words, we are approaching the day that we celebrate as Easter. Easter is not about the bunny and the eggs. It is about the power of God's love sent to us through His son, who gave His life in order for us to have eternal life. Easter is the celebration of His resurrection from the dead. This is the greatest display of the power of the Father's love we will ever know. God the Father demonstrated His love in this for us.

He said to us, I love you this much: that I will let you kill My son for your sin, and then I will raise Him from the dead so that you also can be raised from the dead, that your life can be resurrected for eternity in Him. Paul wrote in 1 Corinthians 6:14, "And God both raised up the Lord and will also raise us up by His power." There is no greater power than that, a love so strong that it brings life to what was dead. This is the resurrection power of His love!

My prayer is that because of His love that He freely gave me, He will use this book and the words He has given me to help you receive His gift of life. So that you may move out of darkness, loneliness, and isolation, as I have, into His marvelous light. His love is our source of power for life, because in our weakness (our lack of power), He is strong. Love never fails and that is why it is the greatest power there is. Paul wrote in 1 Corinthians 13:13, "And now abide faith, hope, love, these three; but the greatest of these is love." In his letter to the Ephesians, Paul prayed for them like this: "that the God of our Lord Jesus Christ, the Father of glory, may give to you the spirit of wisdom and revelation in the knowledge of Him (that they may know Him), the eyes of your understanding being enlightened; that you may know what is the hope of His calling, what are the riches of the glory of His inheritance in the saints, and what is the exceeding greatness of His power (not ours) toward us who believe, according to the working of His mighty power which he worked in Christ when He raised Him from the dead and seated Him at His right hand in the heavenly places, far above all principality and power and might and dominion and every name that is named, not only in this age but also in that which is to come, and He put all things under His feet, and gave Him to be head over all things to the church, which is His body, the fullness of Him who fills all in all." (Ephesians 1:17-23)

Whatever you are lacking, wherever there is a void in your life, He fills all. Whatever seems to have power over you, or against you, He has been placed over and has dominion over -

both in this world and the one to come, so that we might know (again, not with our heads, but in our hearts) what is the hope of His calling and the exceeding greatness of His power toward us who believe, according to the working of His mighty power which He worked in Christ when He raised Him from the dead and seated Him in heaven far above all. This is what Paul experienced when God called him and saved him.

Paul also wrote, "For I am not ashamed of the gospel of Christ, for it is the power of God to salvation for everyone who believes." (Romans 1:16) When God spoke to Saul (later named Paul) for the first time, he heard the Lord, who said to him, "Saul, Why are you persecuting Me?" In essence, the Lord was saying to him "You don't know what you are doing or to whom you are doing it." At that time, Saul was dead in his sins, and he was unaware of it. The Lord spoke to him and basically said, "Hey, what are you doing? Don't you know that when you mess with my kids, you're messing with Me?" Saul had been dragging believers in Christ out of their homes and having them beaten and killed. He was playing for the wrong team in a big way!

But God did not give Saul what he deserved. Instead, He touched him with the power of His love and used him on His team to become one of the greatest apostles in the Bible. This was a demonstration of the power of the Father's love. His love is more powerful than any force that mankind has witnessed, more powerful than earthquakes, floods, tornadoes, hurricanes, tsunamis, bombs, nuclear missiles, hate, or unforgiveness. These all have power to destroy and to kill, but none of them can give life to the dead.

Before I knew Jesus as my savior, I was not the son, brother, husband, or father I was created to be. I didn't know love. Much like Saul, I was playing for the wrong team, just as Paul wrote of the church in Ephesus. In Ephesians 2:1, Paul wrote "And you He made alive, who were dead in trespasses and sins." I was dead in my sins, meaning I was no good to the kingdom of God. Like Paul I was playing for the wrong team, but now the One who is above all in the kingdom lives in my heart and now I live for Him. He works in me to do His good works, not mine. He has forgiven me and brought me back to life by the resurrection power of His love, the power of the Father's love. I pray that He has done that for you, that you would experience the fullness of His love. I ask the Father in the name above all names, the name of Jesus Christ our Lord and Savior. Thank You, Father, that You have heard my prayer.

Chapter Twelve

The Authority of a Father's Love

A s a child, I can remember accepting the authority of my father and mother. I did not understand anything about it, but somehow I knew they had authority over me. I can remember that my father's word was the final authority, If, he said, "you will not leave the table until you clean your plate," you didn't. I had no problem with this one; I got it: "just eat it all and I'm on my way." However, I had a brother, step brothers, and a step sister who didn't catch on to this one real quick, so consequently, I would be back watching television or doing my homework while they were still at the dinner table picking at their food, sometimes even crying about having to eat something they didn't like. Which seemed to me like a total waste of time.

Chores were much the same way. I learned that when my father gave us chores to do, it was best to get after them and get them done because you weren't going to do what you wanted to do until they were done, so again I thought, *Why waste time? Just do it and move one."* This, of course, made my life pretty easy; I guess you could say I was cooperating with my father, who was the authority in my life. Of course, I had no idea at the time that these things he had me do were somehow good for me. I just knew the quicker I did what he asked, the quicker I could get back to my own agenda. Many years later, I came to realize that most of those things he asked me to do were in fact good for me - even better for me than what I would have chosen to do.

Consequently, I acquired some good habits from my early training, such as a good work ethic; I understood there is a time to work and a time to play. You can do both, but just not when you feel like it, but nevertheless a time for both.

Later in my life, as girls, motorcycles, cars, movies, friends and the many other things I could have chosen to do began to increase, I began to struggle with surrendering to my father's authority. Maybe it was the time thing again, now with so much to do, how could I still do it all if I took time to do what my father said? More likely, however, it was just that I wanted to do what I wanted. After all, I was not working full time. I knew how to make it on my own. (Isn't it amazing how smart kids are when they become teenagers!) I thought, *All I've got to do is work, and then play - life is easy!* This attitude of deciding to do what I wanted rather than what my parents told me to do caused something to happen, and I didn't even recognize what was happening.

Life was not easy; in fact, it was much harder doing things my own way than when I was in my father's house, doing things his way. In those days, I just did what he said. He provided all my necessities, and life was good. But when I began doing things my way, life was not easy. In fact, there were many problems and troubles that came, and I had no instructions or experiences to look to for guidance. Consequently, I did what most of us do in a situation that we don't know what to do: We just "wing it" - you know, just guess, do what feels right and seems right. I'm reminded once again of a verse in Proverbs that is so important for us to understand that it is repeated twice in Proverbs, not in different words, but precisely the same. Proverbs 14:12 and 16:25 say, "There is a way that seems right to a man, but its end is the way of death." When I faced problems and circumstances in life that I did not know what to do, I just did what seemed right to me. And just as the verse says, its end was the way of death.

As I began living life according to my own way, (what seemed and felt right, and what the world around me was doing) the more trouble I had. Because I made many decisions this way, I was nearly killed several times, was involved in multiple car accidents, suffered disease, and more. I also caused others in my family much pain.

You may be thinking, *Why didn't you die, John?* There are actually two answers to that question. One, in the natural physical sense, I should have been dead a few times, but it didn't happen. Were they miracles? I used to think I was lucky - you know, sort of right place at just the right time. For example, many years ago when I was about twenty-one, I took a trip from Tulsa to Austin, Texas with three of my friends. On the way back, we met some girls and spent some time with them, leaving Dallas pretty late in the night. We'd been drinking quite a bit earlier in the night and smoked some marijuana; as I remember, we were all in pretty good shape. I drove the first leg out of Dallas, to just a few miles south of Atoka, Oklahoma. At that point I realized I was too tired to drive any further, so I asked if anyone was up to taking over. The oldest man in the car spoke up, so I stopped and let him take over. I got into the passenger seat and went right to sleep.

Within a half hour, I woke up to a loud noise that I'd never heard before. Although I didn't know it at first, I eventually realized it was a saw, called the jaws of life. We'd been in a car accident and the rescuers were working to get us out of the car. I could hear heavy breathing behind me - I immediately wondered how my friends were as I tried to imagine what was happening. I wasn't talking, just thinking. I couldn't see much, except shadows and beams of partial light coming through a small opening a little above me. I just waited, expecting that eventually they would get to me. My back was hurting, and I wanted to stretch or move, but couldn't move much at all. After a while, I noticed the noise had stopped and I couldn't hear anyone near or in the car anymore. I began to realize that they didn't know I was in the car. They couldn't see me. It turned out I was curled up in a tight ball under what was left of the dash. The motor and the front end of the car were gone. We had hit an eighteen-wheeler head on. I began trying to get my hand up to the small hole of light above me. I stuck my hand through that opening and began trying to call for help.

A highway patrolman who was standing next to the wrecker that was winching the car on to the wrecker noticed my hand. He yelled, "Hey, there is still someone in the car!" So, they came back and cut me out. They took me to the hospital in Atoka where they had taken my friends. I recognized the heavy breathing I had heard in the car. Later, they came and told me I was going to be rushed to Tulsa because they couldn't do much for me there. None of my friends survived that night. The doctors in Tulsa told my family that I probably would not make it through the night, but that if I did, I would probably recover. I did, and I did. For years, I wondered, *Why was I spared?* I still do occasionally.

This is just one of many close calls in my life. Was it luck? I think not. I believe it was nothing short of a miracle. I'm sure the families of my friends have asked why there wasn't a miracle for their loved one. I have asked that many times over the years, and I've never heard an answer. Perhaps, it's because it's not the right question to ask. A better question would be *Why were we there at that time? Why was the truck there? Why did we not ask our Father if we should go to Austin?* These are questions I can only attempt to answer for myself alone. I was there because it seemed right to me. The truck driver was working to make a living for his family. I did not ask my Father if I should go because I was the authority in my life, not my Father. My physical father would have said "be careful." And, I did not know my Heavenly Father at that time.

Would things have been different had I known my Heavenly Father? I'd like to think so, however, I'm not totally convinced they would have been different. I'll explain: I'm no different than many of those people in the stories of the Bible. To know God is one thing, but that does not mean you will choose to surrender to His authority or be motivated by the authority of His love. Why do I say this? Well, as I explained, I've struggled with authority. When I surrendered my life to Jesus, I was saying I need You to control my life. I've not done well with running it myself. I said it by faith and received His love by faith. I noticed an immediate change on the inside of me. I was more compassionate toward others, but I did not immediately know how to receive this kind of love. Our relationship with the Father is this way. To know Him is not the same as knowing His nature, His desires, what He wants for us, how He cares for us, how He provides for us, how He intercedes for us, how He and only He can comfort the broken hearted. These attributes are all a part of His divine nature: love.

When people know that those in authority in their lives want only what's best for them, it is much easier to submit to that authority. The only way that comes is through experience. It is not something you can purchase and possess - you must accept it by faith and act on it by faith. When I received this God kind of love in my heart, as I said, I didn't know what to do with it. I began to find out by looking into God's word on a daily basis. This doesn't happen overnight. There is much to read, and even if you read it several times, if you don't spend time in quiet meditation with God, conversation with Him, you will develop your own opinions and ways. Remember, we all know that hasn't worked so well for us before.

The idea here is simple, but hard for us to swallow, surrendering to authority. It's like that awful medicine your mom, aunt, or grandma used to make you swallow. We think, *If it tastes this bad, how could it be good for me?* In much the same way, we feel like surrendering the authority of our life can't be good if it doesn't seem so. We have followed our own feelings and emotions for so long it's hard for us to change.

Over the years, as I continued seeking God in His word, I slowly began to think differently, and consequently to act differently in the midst of life's challenges. This is what the Bible refers to as being transformed by the renewing of our mind. Romans 12:2 says, "And do not be conformed to this world, but be transformed by the renewing of your mind, that you may prove what is that good and acceptable and perfect will of God." As I learned about God's will through His word by spending time each day with Him, the more I began to think about His word compared to the way the world does things. I began to trust His word as the final authority in my life, just as I once did as a child with my natural father, rather than trusting my feelings and emotions. Only by trusting and doing what it says, however, did I begin to realize that God's word truly works in every situation. God's word is true.

I want to give you some examples of how I trusted, or watched someone else trust, God's word more than feelings and emotions. I'll start with one of my personal experiences. I am a homebuilder by trade, and often I have to get my subcontractors to do something a bit differently than their norm, either at the request of my customers, or because I find fault with what they have done. Normally, this is not a problem; usually I point something out to them as nicely and politely as I can. I never tell them to do anything "because I said so, I'm the boss" - at least it never starts that way. A particular incident that comes to mind is one in which I had hired a trim carpenter when my normal guy couldn't get to the job soon enough. This young man had approached me with pretty good credentials. He had a list of builders he had worked for and he had no problem letting me know he was a Christian. I thought it was a pretty good idea to hire this man. I did, and overall, he did a pretty good job. However, the stairs were wood, which requires some extra care to avoid squeaks and movement. I called the young man and asked him to meet me at the job so I could point out a couple of things to him. He agreed to meet me, and when he did, I pointed out that the stair treads were squeaking and needed attention. I asked if he had used shims, glue, and screws. He replied something to the effect of "No, we never do." As I explained what I believed was the proper way to install the treads, he began to blame the framing contractor for the problem. In my mind, this was nothing more than an excuse. I was beginning to feel very angry.

At the time, I was teaching a Sunday school class, and had been studying God's word very regularly. I knew the Bible says, "You have heard it said, 'You shall love your neighbor and hate your enemy,' but I say to you love your enemies, bless those who curse you, do good to those who hate you, and pray for those who spitefully use you and persecute you, that you may be sons of your Father in heaven; for He makes His sun rise on the evil and on the good, and sends rain on the just and on the unjust. For if you love those who love you, what reward have you? Do not even the tax collectors do the same?" (Matthew 5:43-46)

This guy refused to fix the stairs; he looked at me, agreed there was a problem, but told me flatly he was not going to do anything about it. Everything inside me wanted to pay him back. I could see myself jumping on him and settling this: I wanted to knock him down, pounce on him and pound some respect into this young Christian! I could see him lying on the ground in front of that home, hurting. But, fortunately, I chose God's word over those feelings and emotions. I walked him to the front door and closed it behind him. I prayed for the young man and confessed my anger to the Lord. I then had to hire my regular guy to fix the stairs.

The following Saturday morning, just after I had finished my quiet time with the Lord, my cell phone rang. It was the trim carpenter that I had wanted to knock out earlier in the week. He said he had just been in his prayer time and the Lord had spoken to him and said something like "I don't appreciate the way you have treated one of my sons." So, he called and apologized. This, of course, did not pay the cost of the stair repair; however, it confirmed for me that God's word is true. I was moved by his call: it was a personal affirmation to me from God that He knew I had done what His word says instead of what I wanted so badly to do. That affirmation was worth every dime the incident had cost.

Of course, the young man had not done what he should have done according to God's word, so the Lord let him know and he was obedient and called me to apologize. I have to confess, of course, I've been guilty of being in the young man's shoes many times. Renewing our minds to the word of God is a process. We must first get the Word in us and then do it, applying it to our situation.

Proverbs 10:17 also explains this process. "He who keeps instruction is in the way of life, but he who refuses correction goes astray." To keep the word, you heard from God is to do it, instead of choosing the way of the world, which is to do what feels or seems right, which causes us to stray. If the refusal of correction is what causes us to stray, the question becomes, "why do we refuse correction?" I believe it is because we do not understand the authority of a Father's love.

The Bible says, "Love never fails." (1 Corinthians 13:8) You might be thinking, *Really? I loved so and so and they let me down. I gave them all I had and they want nothing to do with me.*

Or, you may be thinking, *I tried to love so and so, I really wanted to, but I guess I just didn't.* Or, *my mom loved my dad, but he treated her badly and then left her.* Or, *I loved my mom, but she left us. I love my daughter, but she won't return my calls. I loved my child and he or she left home, and I don't know where he or she is. What do you mean, "love never fails"; it sure looks like it does.*

I believe this scripture is referring to the God kind of love. His kind of love is completely unconditional. His love is not like what most of us think of as love. The scriptures say this about the nature of God's love: Love suffers long, and is kind, love does not envy, love does not parade itself, is not puffed up; does not behave rudely does not seek its own, is not provoked, thinks no evil; does not rejoice in iniquity, but rejoices in the truth; bears all things, believes all things, hopes all things, endures all things. Love never fails." (1 Corinthians 13:4-7)

I don't know about you, but I didn't make it past the first definition, "love suffers long." The point is none of us are capable of this kind of love. The last one, "Love never fails," is an amazing statement and points to authority. If something never fails, it wins, it rules and is victorious in the end. If that is the case, then we can say it is the final authority, because everything else fails. Only God's love never fails. This is something many of us cannot understand until we receive it. Why is that? It's because we have never experienced it prior to receiving His love. Yes, our parents and grandparents may have done their best, but even the best of them couldn't fulfill the list of characteristics listed in 1 Corinthians 13. I challenge you to think through that list for a few minutes. If you do, I believe you will see that no man or woman can love like that. Sorry, moms and dads! You can try to love on your own, but it will fail.

Here's what I have come to know about the authority of the Father's love. Love never fails. God is love (He never fails.) "In the beginning was the Word and the Word was with God and the Word was God. He was in the beginning with God. All things were made through Him, and without Him nothing was made that was made. In Him was life, and the life was the light of men. And the light shines in the darkness, and the darkness did not comprehend it." (John 1:1-5) What does all that mean to you and me? It means, in the beginning (before anything, including time), Jesus was with God the Father Who is Spirit (John 4:24) and they (Father, Spirit, Son) created us in their image and likeness. (Genesis 1:26) The fact that they ... God ... created us, should point to their authority, but then He (They) said, let them have dominion over everything I (We) created. Normally, one who gives authority to someone must first have it to give it, wouldn't you agree? You cannot give what you don't have. Correct?

This is why you can't love as God loves until you have it. You cannot give it because you cannot give what you do not have. This is why darkness could not comprehend the light. Darkness did not receive the light but darkness contrasts light. Until I received God's love, I was not capable of love. I was in darkness and isolation where nothing is, just me and darkness - not able to receive because of darkness and not able to give because of darkness.

But God had a plan. That plan was love and love never fails. God so loved the world that He gave His only begotten Son, that whoever believes in Him shall not perish, but have everlasting life." (John 3:16) So God sent Jesus to die for you and me because of His love, not because we deserved it (Romans 5:8), but in order to demonstrate His love. The Bible says, "The wages of sin is death," (Romans 6:23), but the gift of God is eternal life in Christ Jesus our Lord." What we deserve is death, but we received a gift instead of what we deserved. When is the last time you were mistreated or ignored by someone, and you responded by giving him or her a gift? God the Father sent Jesus, His Son, to die for us in spite of what we deserve. And because of His gift of eternal life in Christ Jesus, all authority has been given to Him. (Matthew 28:18)

If you know that medicine is good for you, you will most likely take it. Likewise, it is the authority of the Father's love that you must receive and take in order to have the life that He came to give you. Until you receive it, it is not a gift. It must be received. I cannot convince you of His love, nor can I explain with simple words the amazing gift of Jesus (love). It can only be received by faith. Paul writes in Romans 10:8-10, "But what does it say, 'The word is near you, in your mouth and in your heart,' that is the word of faith which we preach; that if you confess with your mouth the Lord Jesus and believe in your heart that God has raised Him from the dead, you will be saved. For with the heart one believes unto righteousness, and with the mouth confession is made unto salvation, for the Scripture says, whoever believes on Him will not be put to shame." This is how you receive the gift: You believe in your heart (not your head) and you say it with your mouth, (not think it).

I don't know about you, but I'm glad we don't have to believe with our head, because it's hard to believe in something with our head that we cannot see with our eyes or touch with our hands. But in our hearts, we can believe. Many of us have put our trust (to believe in means to trust in) all kinds of things and people. But at some point, they all fail. These are all things we see and can touch - people, money, jobs, investments, etc. But God's love can only be received by faith in the One who gave His life for us, in order that we might have and enjoy life. (John 14:6, John 10:10) No one but God Himself can give us life. If He is knocking on your heart, answer the door! Open it and invite Jesus to come into your heart and make you the person He created you to be. God will not make you or force you to do this;

it is entirely up to you because love is patient, doesn't envy, is kind, is not rude, does not parade itself, is not puffed up, does not seek its own, believes, hopes and endures all things, and never fails.

After I received God's love, I wanted to give it to others, but truly, I cannot. I can only tell you that I have received it, and how through Him I can love others the way He first loved me. But only the authority of the Father's love can do this It never fails. Surrendering to His authority, is the source of the power of His love!

Chapter Thirteen

Faith from the Father

The previous chapters describe some of the innumerable ways God the Father reveals His love to us. I have come to know that His love is a gift - remember, fathers give. Ephesians 2:8,9 says, "For by grace you have been saved through faith, and that not of yourselves, it is the gift of God, not of works, lest anyone should boast." Notice, you did nothing to earn this gift. You have nothing to do with it. Notice it also says through faith, not of yourself. Paul writes in Romans 12:3, "For I say, through the grace given to me, to everyone who is among you, not to think more highly than he ought to think but to think soberly, as God has dealt to each one a measure of faith."

In the original language, this would say, *the* measure of faith. The gift of faith is available to everyone because it has already been given. Now, it must be received to really accomplish what it is intended for. Faith must be acted upon to be what it is intended for. The reason the original text says "the measure" is because the Bible teaches that it does not take a huge amount of faith. Yes, the Bible does distinguish between great faith, little faith, shipwrecked faith, etc., but it does not say you need great faith. Matthew 17:20 illustrates this. In response to the disciples' question "Why could we not cast it out?" when they had been unable to cast out a demon, Jesus said, "Because of your unbelief; for assuredly I say to you, if you have faith as a mustard seed, you will say to this mountain, 'Move from here to there' and it will move; and nothing will be impossible for you."

What does He mean by the phrase, "your unbelief?" Is it that they don't believe it is possible for that to happen? I don't think so; that would put a pretty tough burden on them. It would mean it was up to them to have enough faith to do it, which might seem hard for many. A mustard seed is extremely small but as it grows, it produces a great plant loaded with seed. That's why Jesus uses it in this illustration because their part (and ours) is extremely small, like that mustard seed. He knows what we are capable of. Jesus explains this in his interpretation of faith, found in Mark 11:22. "So Jesus answered them and said to them, "have faith in God." He's trying to tell His disciples their faith (belief, trust) is to be in God and His word, not in their own ability to believe something can be done, but that God will do what He says. It is in His ability and authority that we must have our faith.

Jeremiah 1:12 says, "Then the Lord said to me, you have seen well, for I am ready to perform My word." The Father is saying to and through the prophet to us, that He will perform His word, (not our words, and not us performing it.) *Our faith is to be in Him.* Hebrews 11:6 says, "But without faith it is impossible to please Him for he who comes to God must believe that He is, and that He is a rewarder of those who diligently seek Him." This means not only must you believe He exists (although that part is obvious), more importantly it means you have faith that He is God. This is His kingdom and He rules over it, meaning it is through Him and from Him that all things were and are done according to His will. 1 John 5:14,15 says, "Now this is the confidence that we have in Him, that if we ask anything according to His will, He hears us. And if we know that He hears us whatever we ask, we know that we have the petitions that we have asked of Him."

You might be thinking, *How do I know His will?* Maybe you've heard someone say "Who can know what God's will is?" This is why God gave us His will in written form, so we could study it and He by His Spirit reveals and confirms His will and word to us. You know that in the world today we have what we call a "last will and testament," usually left by fathers or parents to their children and sometimes their children's children. This is exactly what we have in God the Father's written will and testament, the Holy Bible. We have story after story of how God the Father has worked in the lives of His children. Some are stories of men and women who followed Him and others are stories of those who didn't follow Him. Both reveal His will for His children. In both instances, faith was essential. This might sound odd to say this but let me explain.

In the Biblical sense of the word "faith," as the previous scriptures describe, our faith is to be in God. However, as I stated above, those who did not follow Him also acted in faith, though their faith was in something else, such as themselves, their intellect, another god, such as money, health, kids, creation, beauty, their circumstances, their emotions, etc. A good Biblical example of this would be the story of the tower of Babel, found in Genesis, chapter 11. The people had decided to build a city for themselves, and in it a tower whose top would reach the heavens. They had faith they could do this, and they were right, they could. The Lord said, in verse 6, "Indeed the people are one and they have one language, and this is what they begin to do, now nothing that they propose to do will be withheld from them." In other words, they all believe they can do this, they have faith they can do this. They are right, because they are of the same mind and speaking the same language, they can and they will. However, it ultimately was not God's will for them to build their own city, so He confused their language so they could not accomplish it. The point is this: Their faith (belief) that they could do this meant they could, but their faith was in their own ability, not in God's. It is true that men can build cities and they continue to try to reach the heavens with them, but they don't last - they are temporary.

In our world, we see countless examples of men's faith in their own ability to gain wealth and success, many times a great deal of wealth and notoriety. Names such as Rockefeller, Hughes, Gates, Trump, etc. all achieved wealth, but none of them has or will be able to keep it forever, and I'm pretty sure their wealth did not give them what they were looking for. In the world we live in wealth and notoriety can be gone overnight, as some have experienced, especially in today's economy. There have been those who were born very beautiful on the outside and continued working on their outward beauty. They won contests and movie roles, but beauty, too, faded. All of these had faith in what they were doing, and it worked; at least, for a time it worked, but there came a time or will come a time when it will no longer work. You cannot keep your outward beauty forever, nor can you take your success and wealth with you when your time is up.

If these things are all temporary, just how much of our lives should we invest in chasing after them? Should they be our main focus, should they consume our time, our lives? It seems that every investor is looking for long-term payoffs, something that will last, that will stand the test of time and continue to grow their wealth. The latest investment craze has once again become gold. We are told it is what we should invest in now, and it is the only investment that is safe. Many have faith that it is, and it has had a steady increase in value for several years, but will it last? Can I take it with me? No, and no. I could leave it to my children and my children's children, but will they be able to take it with them? No. The reality is that while it is good to leave wealth to our families, it would be far better to leave them something that would provide for them forever, would it not?

You might be thinking, *What, can I leave my children, and my loved ones? - What is something that will last forever?* What can I do? Remember, our part is small, like the mustard seed. If you don't understand this principle, you are going to struggle. The hard part is *not* on our shoulders. Personally, I have struggled with this for years thinking about all the mistakes I have made and what I can do to correct them. How can I fix it? What must I do? How can I convince them of my love? How can I do this for them? How can I love them? That's seven "I's" and I could keep going, but you get the picture: "I" puts it all on my shoulders. It's a bad plan, it won't work.

The truth is I must have faith in God, just as Jesus answered the disciples in Mark 11:22; that is it. I'm not to put all my faith in myself or other men or women and our abilities, but in God. I'm pretty sure that when the Father spoke to Abram and told him to get out of his country, leaving his family and his father's house to go to a land that He would show him, Abram must have thought, *But I like it here and I'm used to things around here. I know how to get along here. I can do just fine here. Why should I leave my family and my country?* But the Father also said, "I will make you a great nation; I will bless you and make your name great; and you shall be a blessing. I will bless those who bless you, and I will curse him who curses you; and in you all of the families of the earth shall be blessed."

So, the scriptures say that Abram departed as the Lord had spoken to him. It also says that he was seventy-five when he departed. Wow! I don't know about you, but this seems amazing to me, the fact that at that age, he was willing to go and start a new phase of his life. Of course, he heard from God, but how many who heard something like that from the Father would do it without hesitation? Most of us would first think about ourselves and our families and even how comfortable we are where we are, all the things that we can see and have seen and known. These are the types of things we have learned to put our faith in, but Abram trusted the Father.

Another example is Noah, who built an ark, according to the instructions of the Father, never hesitating even though he had never seen rain or any large body of water, nor a boat or an ark, yet he had faith in what the Father had said. And as a result of trusting in what the Father said, Noah and his family were the only family on earth to be spared the Father's wrath. There are, of course, many other examples of faith in God, as told in Hebrews 11. The common denominator in every story is the person's steadfast faith in the Father, trusting in Him and His word. This is what Jesus meant in Matthew 18:3,4 when He said, "Assuredly, I say to you, unless you are converted and become as little children, you will by no means enter the kingdom of heaven." A child looks to his father for everything - he does not trust in himself for anything because he has not yet learned to provide for himself. Jesus is saying this is the way you have faith in God, like a child you must look to your Father and what He says for everything and every situation.

The Bible describes these men of faith as having a testimony that they walked with God and pleased God. A child that walks with his father is in a safe place. His father will protect him from the things of the world that could hurt the child. He will lead his child in the way he should go, not the wrong way, which would hurt or harm. This pleases the father because he knows his child is safe. Eventually, the child comes to understand what the love of his father is like: it provides for him, protects him, corrects, and teaches him. This is the way we should be with our Heavenly Father, putting our faith in Him and His word. How? It is by faith, just as the verse we started with in this chapter says, "By grace you have been saved through faith, and that not of yourselves; it is the gift of God, not of works, lest anyone should boast." (Ephesians 2:8,9)

Everyone wants to think they are good and have done some good in their lives. That's not necessarily bad; it just won't get you saved. Salvation must be through faith in God (Jesus), not faith in our own abilities to do good deeds. In John 14:6, Jesus says, "I am the way the truth and the life, no one comes to the Father except through Me." Acts 4:12 says, "Nor is there salvation in any other, for there is no other name under heaven given among men by which we must be saved." The apostles Paul and Silas were asked by a jailer, "What must I do to be saved?" They replied, "Believe in the Lord Jesus Christ, and you will be saved, you and your household." (Acts 16:30,31) So this is what we must do if we are to leave our children something that will last forever. Faith in Jesus Christ will outlast wealth, land, homes, or any other gift we might leave them. But you can't give them something you don't have.

This jailer had witnessed something astonishing. Paul and Silas, who had been beaten and thrown into prison, began praying and singing hymns to God. What an amazing display of the power of God's love and of their faith in God. As they were praying and singing, there was a great earthquake that shook the foundations of the prison, and all the doors were opened and everyone's chains were loosed. The jailer woke from a nap and realized that all the doors had been opened. He thought that surely all the prisoners had escaped, so he drew his sword to kill himself. But Paul called out with a loud voice, saying, "Do yourself no harm for we are all here." The jailer called for a light and ran in trembling and fell down before Paul and Silas. He brought them out and said: "Sirs, what must I do to be saved?"

Try to imagine what must have been going through this jailer's mind. First, these two crazies in prison are actually praying and singing after being beaten and thrown in prison. So, he sits back, and falls sleep. Then comes an earthquake, he wakes up in fear, sees the doors opened, and knows he will be killed for allowing the prisoners to escape. In fear for his life, he pulls out his sword and is about to do himself in, when he hears Paul's voice, saying "Don't do it, we're all here!" Now he's really freaked out. He probably thought, *It's dark, how did the prisoner Paul know what I was about do to? Why are they still here? The doors are open. These guys are not normal! There's something really different about them. Why would he care if I killed myself? He could have walked out of here and freed himself, but he was concerned about me. This must be real, this God thing. I need what they have!* So, the jailer ran, fell down in front of them and asked, "What must I do to be saved?" And that's when they told him, "Believe on the Lord Jesus Christ, and you will be saved, you and your household."

In its original text and meaning, this word "believe" meant to rely upon, to put one's trust in, not merely acknowledgement, or credence. In essence he told the jailer you must put your trust in Jesus Christ and rely on Him in order to be saved. Then they spoke the word of the Lord to him and to all who were in his house. The jailer took them the same hour of the night and washed their stripes, their wounds from their beatings. Immediately he and all his family were baptized. When he had brought them into his house, he set food before them, and the Bible tells us he rejoiced, having believed in God with all his household.

Let's review this story: A jailer, probably not a real compassionate guy, winds up believing on the Lord because of an amazing experience with two prisoners, all orchestrated by the Father's love for them, which they had received. That love empowered them to sing praises to the Lord under difficult circumstances and caused them to have compassion on a jailer who probably was not the least bit concerned for their welfare.

Then, when they should have been concerned for their own welfare, they instead put his welfare ahead of their own. By this act of love, they showed God to this jailer, they encouraged him in God's word, and he and his household received their salvation. The jailer instantly became compassionate and ministered to Paul and Silas's needs. Once again, "love never fails!"

Now, back to the subject of faith. Just how much faith to you suppose the jailer had? Not much, I suspect, if we are referring to faith as a noun, faith as something one possesses. If we look at faith as a verb, we see that clearly, when things began to change in his circumstances (the earthquake, fear of being killed by it, and fear of being killed by his ruler for allowing prisoners to escape) he wasn't singing praises to God, and he wasn't thinking of anyone but himself, considering his actions. So how did he get this faith? After hearing the word of God and putting his trust in Him, he was transformed instantly and became a compassionate man, just as Romans 10:17 explains, "So then faith comes by hearing and hearing by the word of God." He and his household were saved, meaning they all received eternal life with God the Father through faith in the Lord Jesus Christ. (John 3:16)

It seems to me that his part of the act of faith he took that day was pretty small, like the mustard seed. It started with a small step of faith, which was simply to rely on Jesus for his life instead of himself, and his own abilities.

If we intend to leave an inheritance to our children and children's children, the kind that will last forever, and never run out, it starts with a very small step of faith we must take in order to pass it on, just as Paul and Silas did, then likewise the jailer did to all his household. This story may not seem like the jailer had childlike faith to you, but here's what I see: Imagine a moment when your child or grandchild, or you in your own childhood were scared. When children are afraid, they run to their parent or grandparent and throw their little arms around their leg and hold on, expecting to be protected, comforted, and provided for. They don't know how they just know somehow their parent will protect them: they always do.

This is what I see this jailer doing, even though he was not a child anymore. He was frightened, afraid for his life and the unknown, and he ran for help. He somehow knew that what he heard and saw in Paul and Silas was something he needed. So, becoming like a child, having this childlike faith was almost instinctive - a response to a desperate situation, motivated by his fear. Faith is the opposite of fear, it overcomes fear, so it was this small childlike step that the jailer took that became the faith to receive his salvation. Jesus did not say you must be a child but become *like* a child. It didn't require a great deal of faith for the jailer to do what he did. He was desperate. He simply knew at that moment he didn't know what to do, and he couldn't rely upon himself.

It doesn't matter whether you are afraid for your life, your job, your kids, your marriage, your bank account, your health, hurting from the loss of a loved one, or hurting because of a broken relationship. It makes no difference your age, how long you've ignored God, or how many other sins you have committed. I was thirty-eight before I began to turn to God for help in my life, and in my late forties before I was truly born again. Revelation 3:20 says "Behold, I stand at the door and knock. If anyone hears my voice and opens the door, I will come in to him and dine with him, and he with Me."

I looked up the meaning of the word "dine" in the original language of the New Testament. It means to break your fast, hence the word we use for breakfast. As I thought more about this, to fast is to give something up for a time or to do without it for a time. I believe that Jesus was in essence saying, *I'm right here knocking at the door of your heart. I'm speaking to your heart, and if you'll hear my voice and open the door, I'll come in to you and your fast will be broken. You won't have to do life anymore without Me, we'll be together.*

If you have not taken this small step of faith of asking Jesus into your heart, a step that will grow and grow and grow, and never run out - if this is the desire of your heart, you have a promise from the Father that He will give you the desire of your heart. The Bible says, "But the word is very near you, in your mouth, and in your heart. (Deuteronomy 30:14) Again, Romans 10:8-10 says, "But what does it say? The word is near you, in your mouth, and in your heart, (that is the word of faith which we preach): That if you confess with your mouth the Lord Jesus and believe in your heart that God has raised Him from the dead, you will be saved. For with the heart one believes unto righteousness, and with the mouth confession is made unto salvation."

Here is a prayer similar to the one I prayed a few years ago that began the transformation of my life:

Father, I realize that I have lived apart from you in sin. I've gone my own way and lived according to my own plans. I need You now. I believe that You loved me so much that You sent Your Son, Jesus, to pay the price for my sins, and that He died for them. I believe You raised Him from the dead and seated Him at Your right hand to be my Lord. Lord Jesus, I need you and I ask You now to come into my heart and make me the person You created me to be. I ask You to be Lord of my life and I thank You, Father, in the name of Jesus. Amen.

You, of course, don't have to pray this exact prayer to receive Jesus as your personal Lord and Savior. You must simply ask the Father by faith in the Lord Jesus to forgive you and accept you, and confess the Lord Jesus as your Lord, and believe in your heart that God the Father has raised Him from the dead to be your Lord. The key is the surrender of the lordship of your life from yourself to Him, through faith in Him, because our Father raised Him from the dead to be our Lord. He alone has the authority to give you eternal life, given to Him by the Father.

This is the small step, the mustard seed of faith, that we must take to be saved. But this is only the beginning of a life of faith that He has created for you, that you should walk in it. It then becomes a life of small steps of childlike faith, trusting in your Heavenly Father in every step you take, a life of faith that obeys God's word, not our own. It is more than just words our faith produces action when we surrender throughout our day to do what He has called us to do. Our faith will produce fruitful works of significance, a meaningful, purposeful life of peace - not free of the troubles of this world yet having peace in every circumstance because we know the love of the Father. We will know peace, just as Paul and Silas experienced this peace when they prayed and sang hymns to the Lord, *and* it produced its fruit: the jailer and his household were saved.

If you prayed to receive Jesus for the first time, or if you prayed to reunite again with the Father, ask Him in the name of Jesus to reveal to you someone you know who is a faithful follower of Christ, and tell that person about your decision. Ask the Father, in the name of Jesus, to direct you to the right church. Seek God daily through prayer and a devotional time spent alone with Him - just you and Him - apart from the distractions of the world. If you do these things, your Father will bless you and lead you in the way you should go, and your faith will grow and grow until your mustard seed of faith becomes great.

Conclusion

Final Thoughts on a Father's Love

When I started this book, I wondered, *Why me?* I guess I knew in part that I would certainly learn from writing it, possibly how to become a better father myself to my children. I thought, *Just maybe this book will help others become better fathers by learning from my mistakes.* I had all kinds of thoughts and questions about how it would play out, and I still do. However, in writing this book, I myself have learned more about the Father's nature - my heavenly Father's nature.

The understanding of His nature is essential to our relationship with Him - not essential to Him, of course, but to us. Just as a child is curious and has many questions, we too, seem to need to understand our Father and His nature. By understanding a person's nature, we can know them better, and understand their motives for the things they do.

If I could use only one word to describe the Father's nature, it would now be the word *selfless.* I believe it describes the nature of God the Father, perhaps better than any other word I can think of. The Holy Bible tells us that He is love. I certainly know and believe that, but until *I knew Him,* my understanding of the word *love* was extremely shallow, at best. By looking at the Bible from the perspective of a Father's love, I have learned much about the nature of my Heavenly Father and it all points to a selfless Father.

In John 1, the Bible explains that "In the beginning was the Word and the Word was with God, and the Word was God. He was in the beginning with God. All things were made through Him and without Him nothing was made. In Him was life and the life was the light of men. And the light shines in the darkness and the darkness did not comprehend it." This used to be somewhat confusing to me. I didn't comprehend it. Here is what I have come to know about these few verses. The Word was first and was with God and was God. He made everything, so before Him and without Him was nothing. Life was in Him and it was the light of men, so it was in Him that we would see, by His light, the life He created us to live, and it was because of darkness in our lives that we could not comprehend the light. The darkness was and is the sin in our lives - that is, simply living our lives according to our own will and way - and that keeps us from the life we were created to live.

The Father gave us His written word to live by in the Old Testament. It was our instructions for this life, but we chose to live according to our own way and not according to His instructions. We chose to live apart from our Father, which is a place of darkness where we can't receive or see the life we were created to live. But the Father did not stop with His written Word. He came to us in human form to be the example and the picture of what we should be. He came through and by His Son, Jesus, sent to us - for us - by the Father's selfless love. Because we, being in darkness, did not comprehend who He was, we rejected Him, and He was crucified, died, and buried. All this was done in our place - for our sins, and the sins of the world, so that we who were in darkness could see the light and live the life He paid for.

But the Father did not stop there: He raised His Son Jesus from the dead by the resurrection power of the Father's love. God made Jesus to be our Lord and the ruler of the Father's kingdom, but again, He was not finished providing for His children. He sent us another, the Holy Spirit, to guide us into all truth and to speak to us the things He has heard from the Father, to tell us of things to come.

The things to come are our next steps, the ones we take one at a time, in order to live this life the Father has provided for us. In John 1:12,13, John writes, "But as many as received Him, to them He gave the right to become children of God, to those who believe in His name; who were born, not of blood nor of the will of the flesh, nor of the will of man, but of God."

The first step of many individual steps to becoming the fathers, mothers, and children we were created to be is to receive the gift of God the Father, which is His Son Jesus, confessing with our mouths and by believing in our hearts the Lordship of Jesus over our lives. Then, and only then, can we begin to live the life we were created to live. Jesus came for us, and to show us how to live a selfless life of serving others, not ourselves. He said, "The Son of Man did not come to be served, but to serve."

As a father, I know I have not served my family the way I should have, but now that Jesus is the Lord of my life, I am equipped to live a selfless life, and I can choose by my free will to live as my Father has shown me. Without Him, nothing was made. He is our source for life. Without Him and before Him was nothing, a meaningless life, one that is self-centered and selfish instead of a selfless life of serving.

I can now take vacations and go where my family wants to go instead of where I want to go. As a father, I am the ruler, or the head, of my house, but I am to rule it by serving my family. As the manager of our business, I am also the one in charge, but the best way to run my business is by serving my customers, my employees, subcontractors, and even my suppliers. As a partner of my church, I serve those in my church family.

No matter what you do or where you do it, this selfless life is the key. Just as it is written, "he who finds his life will lose, it, and he who loses his life for My sake will find it." This is what knowing the Father's love has shown me.

CPSIA information can be obtained
at www.ICGtesting.com
Printed in the USA
FFHW020507061119
55934485-61801FF